D0475345

50 YEARS
OF
AMERICAN AUTOMOBILE DESIGN
1930-1980

DICK NESBITT

Louis Weber, President
Publications International, Ltd.
3841 West Oakton Street
Skokie, Illinois 60076

Permission is never granted for commercial purposes.

ISBN: 0-517-49042-0

This edition published by:
Beekman House
One Park Avenue
New York, New York 10016

Manufactured in the United States of America
10 9 8 7 6 5 4 3 2 1

About the Author

A noted industrial designer and automotive illustrator, Dick Nesbitt graduated with honors from California's prestigious Art Center College of Design (now located in Pasadena), which he attended on a full-tuition scholarship from Ford Motor Company. His extensive professional career includes several years in automotive exterior and interior design at the Ford Design Center in Dearborn, Michigan, and a stint as Senior Special Products Designer for the Texas Instruments Consumer Products Group (calculators and time products) in Dallas, Texas. It was in the latter post that Nesbitt received four patents, including one for the case design of the innovative "Speak 'N Spell" learning aids.

Nesbitt currently resides in Arlington, Texas, where he heads Dick Nesbitt Design Consultants. Formed with a group of associates, this firm has served a variety of clients since 1980. Among its past programs are a complete redesign of Marmon Motor Company's Class 8 conventional and cabover tractor trucks, and advance-design compact buses (24- and 30-foot overall length) for Transit Bus Manufacturing of nearby Fort Worth, Texas. Recent projects include redesigning the "Pargo" electric airport/industrial personnel carriers for Eagle Vehicles, and an array of special truck and van designs for Custom Vehicles Incorporated in Arlington. Nesbitt has developed several unusual CVI products in his capacity as design program manager. These include prototypes for the civilian export version of the Pinzgauer, the high-tech, all-terrain military transport built by Steyr-Daimler-Puch in Austria, as well as an upscale, European-style passenger conversion package for the S-series van range by Iveco of Italy.

The year 1930 is an appropriate point to begin considering the design evolution of the American automobile, for it began the decade that largely established the shape of cars we know today. At the time, few could have predicted the staggering metamorphosis that would occur in those 10 short years. A comparison of the typical 1930 model with its 1939 descendant provides dramatic proof of how complete that transformation was. The peculiar irony is that it all took place during the greatest economic calamity of modern times.

The Wall Street stock market crash of October 1929 touched off a worldwide depression that provided a powerful incentive for car companies to advance the state of their art: survival. With countless thousands of businesses going bankrupt in the early Thirties, millions of workers were left without jobs and thus the means for buying cars. Yet even in the face of unprecedented hardship, many Americans still put a premium on style. And among the many worried auto executives in Detroit, there were a few who recognized that design now loomed as a critical new factor in sales success.

Up to this point, "styling" as we think of it today had yet to be invented, and the basic concepts of automotive design and construction had seen few fundamental changes since the turn of the century. In the early Thirties, most cars were built on a simple, carriage-like chassis rolling on wood-spoke wheels and solid tires. Cart-type leaf springs supported bodies built around multi-piece wooden frameworks, to which metal or treated-fabric panels were attached. Though a variety of new body types appeared in the Teens and Twenties, notably closed styles like the sedan and coupe, traces of carriage design practice were still evident, particularly in the shape of the bodysides and rear end.

All this began changing in the late Twenties, when several forces coalesced to pave the way for the design shift that would be necessitated by the Depression. America's industrial revolution matured in the growing affluence of that wheeler-dealer decade, fueled by the increasing availability of electricity and a host of new labor-saving devices powered by it. Science was unlocking hitherto unfathomable secrets at an accelerating rate in almost every sphere, creating new business opportunities and an even higher standard of living that only served to hasten further discoveries.

This fertile, fast-paced environment spawned a new profession to give form to the many marvelous new functions of science: industrial design. With roots partly in modern art—especially the Art Deco school—and partly in commerce, this hybrid discipline was inspired as much by the need to sell more goods as by the notion that design can make something not only more attractive but, in many cases, more efficient.

Left: A contemporary view of the 1921 Ford Model T center-door sedan shows the traditional four-square styling that prevailed into the early Thirties. Opposite page: Harley Earl's 1927 LaSalle (convertible coupe shown) was the first "styled" car in the modern sense. Note its more rounded overall appearance and "tablespoon" fenders. (Owner: Owen Hoyt)

The shape of today's cars emerged in the Thirties, ironically during the greatest economic calamity of modern times. Few could have predicted back then the vast changes that would occur in car design in the space of just 10 short years.

This logic, plus the high public interest in aviation as a result of World War I, gave rise to the "streamlining" movement, which more or less emerged with industrial design and probably hastened its acceptance as a legitimate field of endeavor. The essence of streamlining was smooth curves and rounded forms imitative of an aircraft's fuselage, a soft sleekness that increasingly came to be associated in the public mind with modern technology and, by extension, superior quality. Once the Depression made the future seem anything by promising for much of society, this style provided a kind of visual escape that strongly implied that tomorrow's world would be far better than today's. This may explain why the streamlined school, with all its game optimism, would dominate industrial design thinking for most of the decade and on into the Forties.

It was almost inevitable that automotive styling would emerge as a specialized branch of industrial design, and it happened relatively early. The year was 1926, when a young artist and body designer for the Don Lee studios in Hollywood, California, signed a consultant's contract with Cadillac at the behest of division general manager Lawrence P. Fisher. The first assignment for Harley J. Earl was to design the LaSalle, the new "companion" make scheduled to arrive in 1927, positioned just below Cadillac on the General Motors price and prestige scale. The result was truly impressive, with an elegance and refinement usually associated only with the most expensive custom bodywork. Indeed, Earl, who had grown up in his father's carriage shop, was inspired by the prestigous coachbuilt Hispano-Suizas of the day. In contrast to its square-rigged contemporaries, the first LaSalle had graceful "tablespoon" fenders, smooth

hood contours, and corners rounded wherever possible. Sedans featured side windows proportioned for a fleeter look, and some models had a hood and cowl painted a darker shade than the main body for greater eye appeal.

On the strength of the new line's high first-year sales, Earl was appointed to es-

tablish a separate styling department within the GM organization, an industry first. He called it the "Art & Colour Section," deliberately choosing the British spelling for "color" to lend an extra dash of class—and, no doubt, credibility—to his pioneering operation.

Earl was a pioneer in many other ways,

and it's not inaccurate to describe him as the father of American car styling. For example, he established the use of modeling clay for evolving the form of various body components, a practice considered highly unusual at the time. Even more significant was his philosophy that a car should be designed as a whole rather than as a collection of individual parts. This contrasted with most custom body builders, who were typically concerned with a car's appearance only from the cowl back, retaining the chassis manufacturer's original hood, radiator, and headlamps pretty much intact. The 1927 LaSalle was the first car to be consciously "styled" in the modern sense, and its strong acceptance proved something that's now taken for granted in Detroit: styling sells.

Most of the design innovations that appeared in the early Thirties originated at the various independent manufacturers and not the "Big Three" of Chrysler Corporation, Ford Motor Company, and General Motors. This is hardly a surprise. With their much smaller size and more

limited resources, the independents had to be more creative to attract customers in that severely depressed market. Then too, the majors could literally afford to be more conservative, so they tended to sit back and watch, letting the smaller outfits try the really advanced ideas and learning from their mistakes.

One of the loveliest and most influential designs of this period was the 1931 Reo Royale, the most ambitious car yet seen from the company formed by Ransom Eli Olds after he sold Olds Motor Works to General Motors. Reo had had fair success with its small, lightweight four- and six-cylinder cars in the Twenties. But sales started tapering off late in the decade, and the firm was in trouble when the Depression hit. As a luxurious "image leader," the Royale was intended to bolster public confidence in the company. Though it was too costly to sell in really high volume, it was a stunning piece of work. Designed by Amos E. Northup, it retained traditional

proportions but had softer, more rounded body surfaces than the then-current norm. Highlights included a smoothed-off windshield header bereft of the commonplace sunvisor, and heavily radiused fenders, with exterior edges rolled under for a smoother look that also eliminated the need for the usual ridged beads. Headlamps were still mounted in freestanding pods, but the pods were elongated, with increased crown on the lens surfaces for better visual integration with the more flowing body and fender contours.

Below: The majestic 1930 Duesenberg Model J dual-cowl phaeton displays the contrasting sweep panel favored by LeBaron and other coachbuilders. Right: Amos Northup's 1931 Model 8-35 Reo Royale (sedan shown) was one of the first attempts at streamlining within the traditional idiom. (Owner: Walter Sprague)

The typical early-Thirties U.S. car "face"

For all the industry's planing and filing, the U.S. car's shape and proportions remained essentially unchanged until the 1934 Chrysler/DeSoto Airflow, the architectural breakthrough.

Hard on the heels of the critically acclaimed Royale came the Graham Blue Streak, another Northup effort displaying a further evolution of his streamlining ideas. Introduced for 1932, it had similarly softened lines, plus several elements that were visually simplified. For example, the lower grille assembly was angled forward to conceal the front chassis components. Fenders were skirted, with the lower edges drawn down almost even with the running boards, which accomplished the same thing in profile. Headlamp pods were mounted directly to the fenders, thus eliminating the need for a separate crossbar, and the radiator grille and shell were tilted back slightly, which suggested speed. All these ideas proved popular and were widely imitated.

For all the industry's planing, filing, and honing in the early Thirties, the basic shape and proportions of the typical U.S. production car remained essentially the same. Although teardrop headlamps, raked radiators, and drawn-down fenders were beginning to make cars look more like cars and less like carriages, the upright, four-square forms of the past persisted.

Then came the breakthrough that forever altered the fundamental architecture of the American automobile. It was, of course, the ill-fated Chrysler and DeSoto Airflow. Bowing publicly at the New York Auto Show in January 1934, it was a collaborative effort involving the renowned engineering team of Carl Breer, Owen Skelton, and Fred Zeder, who were determined to produce the first truly modern production car completely devoid of any preconceived ideas. That they most assuredly did.

The Airflow was dramatically different not only from its conventional contemporaries but from other early attempts at streamlining, in that aircraft design practice dictated much of its construction as well as its styling. Though the body was not, strictly speaking, integral with the chassis, it was engineered, according to Chrysler, "like a modern bridge." Massive longitudinal girders around the engine flowed back into the door frame assembly and roof rails, which in turn were welded to the rear body side rails. The entire assembly was then cross-trussed with smaller horizontal and longitudinal members, creating a cage-like structure claimed to have 40 times the torsional stiffness of ordinary car bodies.

Of course what everyone noticed most about the Airflow was its startling new appearance. Breer had suspected that traditionally styled cars were actually more efficient moving through the air backward than forward, a fact he confirmed with

9

It's likely the Airflow was perceived as "ugly" only _after_ doubts surfaced about its basic design. But though it was an unmitigated sales disappointment, the Airflow was undoubtedly the single most influential car of the Thirties, as competitors proved by imitating it.

extensive wind tunnel tests, assisted by none other than pioneer aviator Orville Wright. He also knew that aircraft were designed around the aerodynamically "pure" teardrop shape, and he began playing with this, modified to allow for a hood and windshield, as the basis for the eventual Airflow. At one point, Breer considered a rear-engine layout as a way to minimize frontal protrusions and thus further reduce wind resistance, but the resulting quirky handling characteristics offset this advantage. The Airflow thus arrived with a conventional engine mounted in front, only it was moved some 20 inches ahead of its usual location. This allowed the back seat to come down from its usual perch atop the rear axle so that all passengers could sit squarely within the wheelbase, where the ride is smoothest in any vehicle. With this seating and drive-train placement, it was a simple matter to shape the body around it, a classic example of "form follows function."

The Airflow was not beautiful, though a high number of initial orders suggests that a number of would-be buyers actually liked the styling. The front end was easily its biggest flaw: too short and stubby relative to overall body length, aggravated by a somewhat featureless, rounded-down nose with a simple "waterfall" vertical-bar grille and fully integral headlamps. In today's vernacular, we'd say the Airflow lacked an "important face." Chrysler itself recognized the problem, giving the 1935 and later models a more pronounced snout, and even going so far as to offer this as a bolt-on kit for the 1934 models, a hasty response to the critics.

As most enthusiasts know, the Airflow was an unmitigated sales disappointment. Debate still rages over what part the unusual styling played in this. Some histori-

ans believe that a bungled introduction was probably as much to blame. A critical four-month delay between announcement and the start of production, plus the assembly line bugs that usually plague a brand-new design, led to ill-founded rumors that the Airflow was a lemon despite its many sterling qualities: superb ride, generous interior space, exceptional performance, surprising economy, and the greater safety of the unitized all-steel body. It's likely the styling was perceived as "ugly" only _after_ the doubts surfaced. In any case, the Airflow would never live down its reputation as a "loser," and that's a pity. It was undoubtedly the single most influential automobile of the decade, as competitors were about to prove by imitation, that sincerest form of flattery.

The Airflow's most obvious imitator was the Lincoln Zephyr, introduced for 1936 as a lower-priced running mate to the big, slow-selling coachbuilt models from Ford Motor Company's prestige division. Work on this "junior edition" had begun in 1932, when company president Edsel Ford got a look at a radical rear-engine design called the Sterkenberg. It was the brainchild of Dutch-born engineer John Tjaarda, then employed by Briggs Manufacturing Company, which Edsel had contracted with some years earlier to supply coachwork for the big V-8 and V-12 Lincoln chassis. The concept involved a definite teardrop body envelope and fully unitized, aircraft-type construction, but Tjaarda's prototype didn't suit the aesthetically astute Edsel, particularly its stubby front end. Still, he

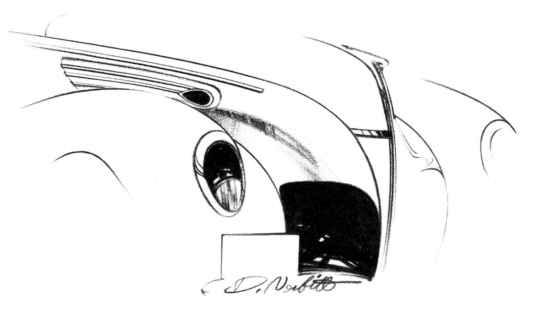

Above: Lincoln's Zephyr appeared two years after the Airflow but sold relatively better, due in part to its more prominent "face" and resulting better overall proportions. (Owner: Harold Hofferber) Opposite page: Bob Gregorie's extensive 1938 Zephyr facelift began the trend toward more horizontal front-end styling, which gained momentum in the early Forties.

was sufficiently intrigued to order further development as a possible basis for Lincoln's new medium-priced Depression-fighter, and turned over the project to his youthful chief designer, Eugene T. "Bob" Gregorie.

After considerable study, including several public surveys, Tjaarda's rear-engine layout was discarded for a conventional arrangement. This came mainly at the insistence of company founder Henry Ford, who felt buyers simply wouldn't take to a power unit at the "wrong end." Edsel thought every Lincoln should have a V-12, but none of the existing units would fit the proposed package. Accordingly, he ordered engine designer Frank Johnson to come up with a 12-cylinder extension of the firm's recently introduced flathead V-8. Gregorie took advantage of this to sculpt a sharply pointed prow, which gave the Zephyr more pleasing proportions than the Airflow. Complementing it was a slightly raked grille composed of fine horizontal bars, swept up at its upper rear corners to match the shape of the vee'd "alligator" (one-piece rear-hinged) hood. As on the Airflow, headlamps were nestled

snugly in the front fenders, though they were higher, more widely spaced, and more upright. The two cars were remarkably similar from the cowl back, however, with the same kind of fastback roofline, rounded body contours, and ovoid side window shaping.

For all its newness, the Zephyr was quite old-fashioned in several important areas. Despite the strong, lightweight body/chassis engineering and less air drag than the Airflow (though the Zephyr was not extensively tested in the wind tunnel), it delivered adequate rather than sparkling performance, mainly due to the mild-mannered engine. Worse, the V-12 lacked the refinement expected in multi-cylinder engines and quickly developed a reputation for oiling troubles. Finally, production economics and Henry Ford's stubbornness dictated that the Zephyr use the same antiquated suspension as a Model T, a solid axle riding on a transversely mounted leaf spring at each end, and mechanical brakes instead of the increasingly common hydraulic systems.

Nevertheless, the Zephyr succeeded where the Airflow failed. It sold in numbers previously unheard of at Lincoln, thus assuring the marque's survival at a time when most other luxury makes were on the ropes. In fact, the Zephyr would be Lincoln's only product after 1939, a heavily modified version of the original design that would carry all the way through 1948.

Industry-leading General Motors took a much more evolutionary approach to streamlining throughout its corporate lineup. Advanced though they were, the Airflow and Zephyr weren't really typical of their makers' products as a whole, and it took several years for their forward-thinking features to filter down to their linemates. General Motors, on the other hand, had a very carefully structured system in which new design elements appeared first on its more expensive lines—typically Cadillac—then passed down year by year to the lower-priced models even as new ideas were introduced on the upper-end cars. For example, the 1932 Chevrolet sported a radiator shell, optional grille guard, and hoodside door vents that were all quite similar to those on the majestic 1930 Cadillac Sixteen.

LaSalle had been GM's style leader ever

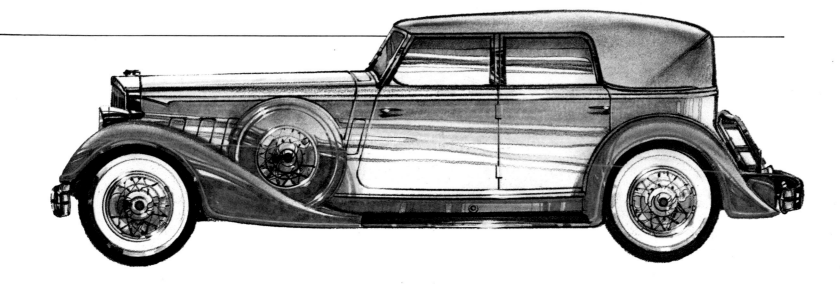

since Harley Earl's masterful 1927 original, and it continued that role for 1934, the year the company began moving toward more noticeably streamlined forms. GM had been thinning its ranks in response to the Depression, eliminating the Viking (Oldsmobile) and Marquette (Buick) companion makes and retaining Pontiac instead of its Oakland parent. This left LaSalle, which was scheduled for termination after 1933. But Earl had a natural fondness for the make, and realized that the decision might be reversed if he could come up with an extraordinary new design. Colleague Jules Argamonte did the rest, and LaSalle was given a reprieve.

What emerged was an exceptionally tasteful amalgam of contemporary streamlining ideas. Earl was often inspired by both aircraft design and the narrow-front, high-speed record cars of the day. The '34 LaSalle reflected this in its slim, vertical radiator—which would be a hallmark of the make through its demise in 1940—and twin-bar "biplane" bumpers (with the blades separated by widely spaced "bullets") created by staff stylist J.R. Morgan. Deeply drawn "pontoon" fenders were

Opposite page: 1936 Lincoln Zephyr. This page, top: 1932 Packard Sport Phaeton. Above: 1934 LaSalle marked General Motors' first move toward streamlining.

General Motors' first big departure from traditional proportions and passenger packaging was the trend-setting 1938 Cadillac Sixty-Special, a landmark design then and now.

joined to the bodysides up front by low-set, neatly faired-in "catwalk" areas decorated by a subtle group of five vertical chrome ribs, providing a highlight detail at the leading edges. Reinforcing the aircraft theme were shapely headlamp pods attached to the radiator shell by horizontal struts that resembled a plane's wing or airfoil. This car was perceived as both modern and aesthetically pleasing and, perhaps predictably, it was a fair commercial success.

GM's first big departure from traditional body proportions and passenger packaging was the trend-setting Cadillac Sixty-Special of 1938. Originally intended as a LaSalle, it was a smaller, somewhat sportier "personal-luxury" sedan aimed at more youthful buyers with a more sophisticated sense of style. It was marketed as a Cadillac because production costs proved higher than expected, thus dictating a stiffer price and, with it, the need for a more prestigious nameplate. Selling a smaller car for more money was quite a gamble for Cadillac, but the handsome styling paid

dividends, and the Sixty-Special was very well received in a customarily conservative area of the market.

The Sixty-Special was primarily the work of Cadillac's young new chief designer William L. Mitchell, and it launched him on an illustrious career at GM Design that would ultimately span some four decades (he succeeded his mentor, Harley Earl, as company design director in 1958). It was a brilliant sendoff. A truly midships passenger compartment afforded the opportunity to establish a new profile, and

this is where the Sixty-Special was most strikingly different. Its top or greenhouse area appeared to be separate from the lower body, which featured an extended rear deck with an integral instead of a detachable trunk. Running boards were conspicuously absent, and glass area was dramatically enlarged, thus going against the small "porthole" windows so typical of mid- to late-Thirties design. The side windows were artfully edged by thin, bright metal frames that gave the car a light, airy appearance not unlike that of a convertible sedan. The roofline and fenders were rectilinear, in contrast to the teardrop shapes prevalent elsewhere.

With its dashing looks and a proven chassis (borrowed from Cadillac's popular V-8 Series 60) the Sixty-Special was a hit. Despite a 25-percent price premium and the availability of just a single body style, it outsold the entire Series 60 line by better than 3 to 1 for 1938. It would do even better in subsequent years, bolstered by additional variants that included division-window and sliding metal sunroof models, the latter an industry first.

Competitors had not been idle, of course. Moving quickly to correct its Airflow mistake, Chrysler Corporation announced "Airstream" styling for a companion group of 1935 Chrysler and DeSoto

Opposite page: 1938 Cadillac Sixty-Special launched William L. Mitchell on his illustrious 40-year career at GM Design. Above: The futuristic 1933 Pierce-Arrow Silver Arrow show car.

models, a less radical approach to streamlining that proved far more saleable. Conceived under the direction of company styling chief Raymond H. Dietrich of Le-Baron coachworks fame, it was also applied to that year's Dodge and Plymouth with good sales results. This corporate look evolved cautiously over the next few years as Chrysler adopted the much more conservative attitude toward design that would characterize its cars until the mid-Fifties.

Ford Motor Company also played it safe in the mid-Thirties, apart from the Lincoln Zephyr, but Bob Gregorie successfully updated that car for 1938. In the process, he set a new styling trend: the horizontal-format front. Though mostly a carryover of the original 1936-37 design, this year's Zephyr wore a more modern face, with low-rise twin grilles flanking a central, body-color vertical divider. Headlamps were now fully absorbed into the front fenders to eliminate the previous "bug-eye" look. Thin horizontal grille bars further accentuated the illusion of width, as did the flatter, less sculptured "catwalk." A complete contrast to the upright LaSalle nose, this lower-and-wider look would be widely imitated.

Also appearing in 1938 was a radical new Graham. Seeking another sales winner as advanced as the now-dated Blue Streak, the firm again called on Amos Northup, who conjured up one of the decade's best remembered but least successful cars, the unmistakable "Spirit of Motion." Its most dubious feature was an aggressive, forward-thrusting front devoid of the usual vertical radiator, a treatment that was soon unflatteringly christened the "sharknose." Hidden door hinges, door handles neatly blended into full-length upper body moldings, and fenders shaped to match the angle of the deeply undercut

nose all contributed to a look that implied speed even with the car at rest. Unfortunately for faltering Graham, the styling was anything but popular, and the "Spirit of Motion" failed to move very quickly from dealer showrooms despite the available performance of the only supercharged engine still in American mass production. In a way, the "sharknose" was the definitive Art Deco car. This may explain why it was well received in France, where the movement had originated in the mid-Twenties. In the U.S., though, it only hastened Graham's demise.

No company produced more Classics relative to its size than Auburn-Cord-Duesenberg. Brought together by flamboyant financier Errett Lobban Cord, these three marques were arguably the finest expressions of American design in the Thirties, and each has a special place in the affections of car lovers today.

By far the most imposing of this trio was the magnificent Duesenberg Model J, announced in the fall of 1928. Everything about it was outsized, from its massive chassis with a "standard" 142.5-inch wheelbase, to its race-bred, 420-cubic-inch Lycoming straight eight with dual overhead camshafts and an advertised 265 horsepower, more than twice that of its nearest contemporary, the 112-bhp Chrysler Imperial eight. As Cord's cost-no-object attempt at the "world's finest motorcar," the Model J was as lavish and expensive as you'd expect. Prices started at $8500, roughly $50,000 in today's money, and that was for the bare chassis. The bodywork was anything the customer desired—and could afford.

America's coachbuilders lavished some of their best efforts on Duesenberg chassis. Particularly memorable are the Le-Baron and the LeGrande dual-cowl phae-

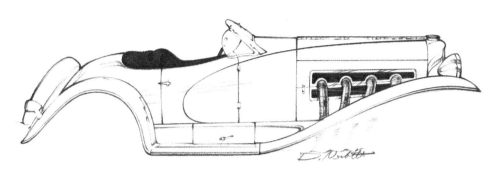

Above: The singular Duesenberg SSJ roadster reduced to its bare essentials. Only two were built. Opposite page: The Combination Coupe in Graham's 1939 "Spirit of Motion" line. This styling bombed badly. (Owner: Les Aubol)

tons with their bodyside "sweep panels." Often finished in a contrasting color, these panels were slightly recessed into the sheetmetal, beginning on the hood as a line either side of the radiator cap, widening at the cowl sides, and ending in a graceful reverse curve at mid-body. Unlike most luxury cars of the period, Duesenberg coachwork had a rakish, high-performance character befitting the make's racing heritage, a legacy of brothers Fred and August Duesenberg. And despite their king-size dimensions, most of these cars avoided the heavy, ponderous look found on so many of their rivals. The trademark Duesenberg radiator, designed by Alan Leamy, remains one of the best-known single features in the history of automotive design, and it inspired similar treatments on the 1931 Chrysler line as well as the first car to bear E.L. Cord's name, the front-wheel-drive L-29.

The Cord destined for design immortality was the 1936-37 810/812, the fabled "coffin-nose." It was the inspired work of former GM staffer Gordon Buehrig, who'd come to A-C-D as chief body designer. The

previous year, Buehrig had convincingly demonstrated his mastery of proportion—not to mention cleverness—by restyling the 1934 Auburn Twelve body from the cowl forward, adding a rakish new radiator and hood, beautifully curved pontoon fenders, and external exhausts. The result was one of the most breathtaking automobiles ever built, the 1935 Auburn Supercharged boattail speedster, long an acknowledged Classic. All of that year's Auburns looked fast, powerful and, most importantly, new. Amazingly, Buehrig accomplished this transformation on a modest $50,000 budget.

The new Cord was a more ambitious project, the first car to bear that name since the L-29's demise in 1932. Because it was originally planned as a new small Duesenberg, it was to be ultra-modern, and Buehrig came up with numerous imaginative touches. Again prefiguring a trend, the expected vertical radiator was replaced by horizontal louvers that wrapped fully from one side of the hood to the other. This was prompted by Buehrig's novel concept of replacing the normal single radiator with

Visual honesty and simplification of form marked Gordon Buehrig's peerless 1936-37 Cord 810/812, long judged a design triumph. It was ultra-modern and imaginative yet tasteful and beautifully balanced.

two smaller units mounted sideways in the catwalk areas. The idea was ultimately abandoned, but the "coffin-nose" front was retained. Another innovation was hidden headlamps, mounted in shapely pontoon front fenders and operated by interior handcranks. This feature wouldn't be widely seen until the mid-Sixties. You can imagine how futuristic it must have seemed in the Thirties.

Visual honesty and simplification of form were evident throughout the second-generation Cord. Door hinges were concealed and running boards discarded, thus highlighting the exquisitely proportioned body and fenders. Taillamps were set flush for the same reason, and the rear license plate was mounted centrally, another break with convention. Even the cover for the forward-mounted transmission was carefully contoured to reflect the components beneath it. Though the two- and four-passenger open body styles were arguably nicer-looking, the 810/812 sedans were nearly as attractive. This wasn't lost on Graham and Hupp, which briefly tried to resurrect the sedan in an abortive attempt at survival in 1939-40. The complexity of the Cord body dies precluded the profitability of either venture. As for

the Cord itself, it perished along with Auburn and Duesenberg when E.L. Cord's shaky business empire collapsed in 1937. Some enthusiasts still mourn the loss, but at least they can be grateful that it didn't happen earlier.

As the Thirties closed, America's automakers could look back on a decade of remarkable design progress. Led by breakthroughs like the Cord 810, Chrysler's Airflows, the Lincoln-Zephyr, and Cadillac's Sixty-Special, the upright boxes of 1930 had quickly evolved into much sleeker forms, riding longer wheelbases

and powered by smoother, more reliable six- and eight-cylinder engines mounted on rubber cushions. Wheels were no longer the spindly, large-diameter wire-laced affairs of old but smaller, stronger, stamped disc types carrying far sturdier "jumbo" tires. Cars were becoming wider

Below and opposite page: The 1937 Cord 812 phaeton. Above: Packard's 1940 convertible victoria by Darrin. Note the smooth "pontoon" fenders.

The early Forties were dominated by extensions of Thirties design trends and the emergence of a new style that went beyond streamlining. The 1940-41 Lincoln Continental is arguably the best example of this "transition" period—timelessly handsome.

as bodies spread outward to absorb separate fenders, and overall height was coming down thanks to chassis and suspension advances. Thus, the American car of 1940 was not only more stylish but smoother-riding—and a good 20 mph faster—than its counterpart of 10 years earlier. It was also safer and more comfortable, with a roomier steel body, wider and plusher seats, greater expanses of glass for superior outward vision, provisions for "windows up" ventilation, more complete and legible instrumentation, and simpler, easier-to-use controls.

The immediate prewar years were dominated by extensions of design trends initiated in the Thirties, even as a new style began to emerge that clearly went beyond streamlining. The original Lincoln Continental of 1940-41 is arguably the single best representative of this transition period—timeless in its appeal, near-flawless in its execution. Conceived by Edsel Ford and brought to life by Bob Gregorie, it was essentially the normal Lincoln Zephyr coupe and convertible reworked with proportions and detailing that Edsel associated with the "thoroughly continental" European grand touring cars he so admired. The decision to proceed

Conceived by Edsel Ford and executed by
Bob Gregorie, the 1940-41 Lincoln
Continental featured long-hood/short-deck
proportions, a prow front, and a revival of
the exposed spare tire.

with a production model was prompted by strong public interest in a prototype convertible that Edsel drove around West Palm Beach, Florida, during his annual winter vacation there in 1939-40.

What set the Continental apart was its rakish long-hood/short-deck proportions. It was obviously a Ford product, with the same sort of split-grille prow used on the company's 1939-40 models, including the new medium-price Mercury line. A hood-line seven inches longer and three inches lower than the normal Zephyr's made all the difference. Adding to the Continental's racy looks was an overall height some three to 10 inches less than on other cars of the period. Bucking contemporary trends, the trunk was emphasized by being noticeably squared off, and the spare tire was brought out of hiding, mounted on the tail in a body-color housing. It was a glamorous package—close-coupled, elegant, understated. The convertible cabriolet featured a top with very wide—and thus blind—rear quarters that furthered the impression of private, personal luxury, while the coupe's thin-frame side window treatment *a la* Cadillac Sixty-Special accomplished much the same thing. Unfortunately, the Continental inherited some of the same faults that plagued the Zephyr, and it was heavier, owing to the considerable extra leading involved in its mostly handbuilt body. Nevertheless, it was a design *tour de force* that cast a glow over an otherwise ordinary Ford Motor Company line. In later years it would be honored by no less an aesthetic arbiter than the prestigious Museum of Modern Art.

At General Motors the orders of the day were increasingly heavy body appearance and lavish use of die-cast and stainless-steel brightwork. Harley Earl had a grasp

of the car buyer's psychological motivations that was unmatched by any other designer, and he knew a chromier, more "substantial" look would make customers feel they were getting more for their money. This perfectly matched the "car for every purse" philosophy of company chairman Alfred P. Sloan, Jr. It also helped solidify GM's dominance in virtually every market sector in these years. The extra exterior ornamentation served three purposes. First, it provided ready distinction among the company's several makes, and models within each division's lineup. Second, it cleverly disguised the use of only a few bodyshells throughout the corporation, where actual sheetmetal differences were confined largely to the fenders and hood area. Finally, it was intended to bolster resale value by drawing the eye away from fading paint and emerging rust on a used model, giving it a brighter appearance that, for most people, implied a higher price than for a less dressy car.

Meantime, GM was leading the indus-

try in integrating fenders with the main body form. The all-new 1942 Buick predicted an inevitable postwar trend with front fenders that flowed all the way back through the central body section to connect with the rear fenders, still of the "pontoon" school but much less prominent. This car was also notable for its much lower grille that stretched almost all the way across the front, a trend also much in evidence at Chrysler Corporation in 1941-42.

One of the Forties' more progressive designs was also one of the most pleasing. It came from a somewhat surprising source: normally conservative Packard. Arriving at mid-model year 1941 was a single four-door sedan called Clipper, designed by the eminent Howard A. "Dutch" Darrin and modified for production by Packard styling chief Werner Gubitz. With its flowing fenders, hidden running boards, tapered tail, and smooth overall lines, it was Packard's first move away from traditional square-rigged lines. It was also very well received—so much so, in fact, that the firm applied Clipper styling to virtually all its 1942 models.

During the war, the public's appetite for new cars was partly slaked by a number of magazine features depicting the bold and futuristic postwar world that, presumably, was just around the victory corner. Typically, these optimistic visions were peppered with cars that looked more like vacuum cleaners, often with clear "bubble" tops made of plastic, that new wonder material, and invariably racing down superhighways toward ultra-modern cities. Some of these stories predicted that the automobile would soon be replaced with low-cost helicopter-like vehicles. Others forecast a myriad of spinoffs from wartime technology, including radar-controlled automatic guidance systems ("no steering!"), turbine engines, 100-mile-per-gallon commuter cars, atomic power, all-plastic cars, and dozens of other fanciful notions. It was a lot of fun, but wildly unrealistic for the most part. And once civilian production resumed in late 1945, the public was only too eager to buy almost anything on wheels. So what if it couldn't fly? What mattered was that it was *new*.

The heady economic conditions in the early postwar years led a number of would-be millionaires to try their hand at the car business, and some of their plans were indeed quite advanced. But few ever progressed beyond a handful of cars—if that far—usually due to poor planning and/or inadequate finances.

The most successful of the newcomers handily avoided these pitfalls to become the nation's leading independent automaker in just three years. It was Kaiser-Frazer Corporation, an uneasy alliance between Joseph Washington Frazer, a 35-year industry sales veteran, and Henry J. Kaiser, the brash west coast ship-

building tycoon. Just before the U.S. entered World War II, Frazer and his associates had acquired the remnants of Graham-Paige Motors with the idea of producing a new postwar model. Frazer was looking for a moneyed partner in early 1945 when he was introduced to Kaiser, whose pockets were bulging from fat wartime contracts. The two acquired Ford's mile-and-a-half-long ex-bomber factory at Willow Run, Michigan, where Henry hoped to build a full-size Kaiser with front-wheel drive, torsion-bar suspension, and unit construction. That car was precluded by unworkable engineering, but the new firm scored big by getting out a more conventional, rear-drive Kaiser and a costlier Frazer companion beginning in June 1946. The basic four-door sedan body was shaped by Dutch Darrin and featured the industry's first true flush-fender styling. The hood was still slightly higher than the front fender tops, which carried back through the beltline to the rear deck. At a time when the majors had only warmed-over prewar models on hand, K-F's cars were fresh and stylish. This plus solid construction, an unheard-of array of colors and trims, and a fine ride, got the company off to a flying start. Unhappily, it began a nosedive soon after takeoff.

Appearing at about the same time was Studebaker's all-new 1947 design, which sparked the question, "Which way is it going?" Though based on concepts developed by the Raymond Loewy team, it's

Opposite page: Separate trunks were still offered even after they were being merged into the main body. Above: 1938 Cadillac Sixty-Special popularized the integral trunk.

Magazines were filled with fanciful "cars of the future" during World War II, but the unprecedented postwar seller's market kept all-new designs from appearing until 1948-49 except for Kaiser, Studebaker, and Tucker.

Packard's 1941-42 Clipper

more properly credited to team member Virgil M. Exner, who influenced the final production styling mainly from the windshield forward. With a shorter hood and a blunter, more ornate front than initially envisioned, the '47 Stude seemed to lack "direction" (even though its rear fenders still stood out from the main body), hence the aforementioned query. However, this styling was quite advanced in many ways, and it remained so even after the majors bowed their first new postwar models for 1949. One body style in particular seemed to have come right off the pages of those wartime magazines: the Starlight coupe, with a severe, four-section wraparound rear window. The new envelope body gave all models excellent passenger room, adding six inches to front seat width and 10 in the rear. Despite the jibes, this design helped Studebaker to its best-ever sales in 1950, and it continued to do well until it was replaced two years later.

The most radical of the early postwar

"wonder" cars was also one of the most controversial automobiles ever built: the Tucker "48." Engineer and erstwhile promoter Preston Tucker was behind this unorthodox rear-engine fastback four-door powered by an air-cooled horizontally opposed six. Free-thinking Alex Tremulis was responsible for the styling, which again harked back to some of those futuristic wartime dream cars. Though all four fenders were separate forms, with no attempt at integration with the main bodyshell, the Tucker was strikingly modern. Its body was an exceptional 79 inches wide, which enhanced a ground-hugging stance made possible by the rear-engine layout. A proud vee'd nose jutted out firmly between severely depressed catwalk areas, and there was a novel center-mounted third headlamp that turned with the front wheels. Below this was a full-width grille capped by a broad U-shaped bumper, matched out back by similar latticework for exhausting engine heat. De-

Opposite page: Kaiser-Frazer (1948 Frazer Manhattan shown) featured the industry's first true flush-fender styling. (Owner: Arthur J. Sabin) This page, top: Studebaker was "first by far with a postwar car" for 1947. Shown is that year's Champion three-passenger coupe. Left: Five-passenger Starlight version boasted this severe wraparound rear window. Above: Tucker "48" doors were cut up into the roof.

spite its dramatic lowness, the Tucker offered outstanding passenger room in a safety-styled interior featuring recessed driver controls, ample crash padding, and a "storm cellar" into which front seaters could dive in the event of an accident. There were many other innovations, including doors cut into the roof for easier entry/exit, a two-piece windshield that popped out harmlessly on impact, and a drivetrain package that could be removed and replaced in only 15 minutes. Performance was terrific: 0-60 mph in 10 seconds, 0-100 mph in 33 seconds, and a top speed of 120+ mph. Aiding the last was a drag coefficient estimated at 0.30, excellent even by today's standards.

Despite all its advances—or maybe because of them—the Tucker didn't get very far. Only 50, mostly hand-built "production" examples were completed at a leased wartime Dodge bomber plant in Chicago before the firm was forced to shut down amid charges of stock and mail fraud. Preston Tucker, who was ultimately tried and acquitted, long defended his car as "too good" and thus a threat to the entrenched Michigan political interests he claimed had shot him down. Still, his breezy promises, short temper, and some carelessness in dealing with government agencies made him a natural target for scrutiny. In the end, he probably hurt his own cause as much as he helped it, but his car would be remembered and many of its features would later be copied.

Back among the mainstream producers, 1948 brought another all-new design that was almost as radical as the Tucker: the now justly famous "Step-down" Hudson. The nickname referred to a passenger compartment floor dropped below the level of the chassis side rails, which extended nearly all the way around the pe-

rimeter of a rigid "Monobilt" body. The result was an exceptionally safe and roomy car with girder-like side-impact protection and a lower center of gravity that afforded superior handling. This concept was developed by Hudson chief stylist Frank Spring and company engineering director Sam Frahm. Though massive and heavy-looking, the new models were nevertheless attractive, with a slab-sided torpedo shape and narrow window openings that made them look like something out of Buck Rogers. A horizontal mid-body character line and covered rear wheels enhanced the long, low appearance.

Innovative though it was, the Step-down, like all unitized cars, was more difficult and costly to change than a conventional body-on-frame design, and sales would never be high enough to pay for more than modest annual styling changes through the last of the line in 1954. Hudson did manage a hardtop coupe for 1951, but it lacked funds for developing a V-8 engine, an important sales weapon in the Fifties, or a hoped-for station wagon, which probably would have sold well. Even so, the Step-down earned a secure place in history with the all-conquering 1951-54 Hornet, which dominated the early years of U.S. stock-car racing.

Also appearing for 1948 were the first of the Big Three's new postwar models. Perhaps predictably, they came from General Motors, now clearly established as the industry's design pacesetter. Ushering in the new corporate look were the top-shelf Oldsmobile series, christened "Futuramic

98," and the entire Cadillac line except for the big Series 75 sedans and limousines. Both exemplified Harley Earl's continuing fascination with aircraft, particularly the Lockheed P-38 "Lightning" twin-boom pursuit (which he and his staff had seen before the war when it was still top secret). Bodies were longer, lower, and wider, accented by smooth "mound" hoods and torpedo-shaped rear fenders. The Oldsmobile sported a simple twin-bar grille in a broad inverted U. Under its headlamps

Opposite page, top: Fastback Tucker "48" was torpedo-shaped. (Owner: David Cammack) Bottom: 1948 Hudson was more slab-sided. (Owner: John Otto) Above: 1948 Cadillac Series 61 sedanet.

were simulated air scoops inspired by the real thing on the P-38's engine nacelles. The fighter's shapely dual rudders prompted the Cadillac's modest tailfins (which the division initially described as "rudder styling"), the start of a trend that would be carried to literally ridiculous heights by the end of the Fifties. Cadillac's fins and Oldsmobile's "rocket" motif are examples of strengthening a make's identity through the use of visual cues, a well-established Detroit practice that would see further development in the years ahead.

One of the most familiar such cues was Packard's distinctive ox-yoke grille, and it was still around on that firm's first new postwar models, which also debuted for '48. This design amounted to an extensive facelift of the original Clipper, but the results were debatable. It was taken from the final version of the Phantom, a one-off landau-roof convertible created in 1941 for company stylist Ed Macauley. The idea was to fill out the bodysides to give the effect of flow-through fenders, but it only added 200 needless pounds and made the Clipper look unfortunately fat. A short, squat rendition of the "ox-yoke" hardly helped. With a certain affection, Packard enthusiasts have long dubbed this generation the "pregnant elephant." More objectively, it was the first of the "inverted bathtub" designs, a style that came to the fore the following year.

The bulk of the industry's new postwar models appeared for 1949, with completely revamped styling from Ford, Chrysler (in the spring of that year), and Nash, plus a new-look Chevrolet, Pontiac, and Buick from GM. Ford Motor Company, then in the midst of a severe cash crisis, decided to release its all new '49 Ford six months ahead of the competition, in June 1948.

The '49 Ford was the result of a crash program decreed by Ernest R. Breech, recruited from Bendix to be second-in-command to recently named company president Henry Ford II. Breech was uncomfortable with Bob Gregorie's proposed Ford styling, fearing it too ponderous to find wide favor. As the firm's recovery would largely hinge on the '49 Ford's acceptance, Breech turned at the last minute to an independent design team led by consultant George Walker. This group's alternative proposal was ultimately accepted, and went into production with surprisingly little change on a 114-inch wheelbase.

Despite its hasty development, the '49

Ford proved very popular, and it literally saved the company's hide. Though Walker usually gets credit for this design, it was largely the work of young Dick Caleal, one of his team members. Assisting him were colleagues Robert Bourke and Holden "Bob" Koto of the Loewy studios at Studebaker, a bit of moonlighting that explains why a bullet-motif front appeared here and on Studebaker's own facelifted 1950 models.

The '49 Ford emerged with full flush-fender bodywork and front fender tops just a little lower than the hood. While the massive severity of the slab sides could have been an aesthetic disaster, the end result was skillfully done and quite at-

Most of Detroit's first new postwar designs appeared for model year 1949, a vintage styling year and one of the busiest in U.S. automotive history.

Opposite page: 1949 Packard Super Eight convertible represents "bathtub" styling. (Owner: Marshall Burton) Below: So does the somewhat sleeker '49 Mercury. (Owner: Bob Ward) Above: 1949 Ford (club coupe shown) was a deftly designed sales winner.

tractive. Large window areas helped counteract the visual heaviness of the lower body, as did a profile that was much more square than the late-Forties norm, with a clearly defined rear deck area. Ornamentation was kept to a minimum and helped support the overall design rather than detract from it. A simple horizontal rub strip in bright stainless steel provided just enough accent for the bodysides, and a modest creaseline running forward from the taillamps provided visual interest at the rear of all models save station wagons. The grille's large central "bullet" or "spinner" was flanked by simple horizontal bars, and the whole assembly seemed to "float" in a cavity that was prominently

peaked in the middle. Offering fine passenger and cargo space within fairly compact dimensions, the '49 Ford was a prime example of the "form follows function" ideal in industrial design.

By contrast, the '49 Mercury and its Lincoln cousins were firmly in the bathtub mold, very smooth and rounded, with low rooflines and shallow windows that accentuated the form's inherent bulkiness. Again, front fenders were lower than the hoodline, flowing back into the mid-body area to help relieve the slab sides. The transition from backlight to rear deck was much less abrupt than on the Ford. Appropriate for these costlier models, grilles were more ornate, though chrome was used sparingly elsewhere. An interesting Lincoln touch was "sunken" headlamps set back slightly from the surrounding sheetmetal.

A more extreme expression of bathtub styling was Nash's new '49 Airflyte. It differed from the Ford products in having a full fastback tail, more fulsome bodysides, and wheels that were semi-skirted at the front as well as the rear. The basic shape is claimed with some authority by Bob Koto, who collaborated with Ted Pietch on a 1943 scale model that looked much like the eventual production design. In an age when wind tunnel testing was still uncommon in Detroit, the Airflyte boasted a total air drag of only 113 pounds at 60 mph, versus up to 171 pounds for contemporary Packards. The result—then, as now—was improved fuel economy. An unhappy drawback was those skirted wheels. The skirts were formed by the lower fender sheetmetal and thus permanent, which made for cumbersome tire changing and a needlessly wide turning circle. Nevertheless, the Airflyte proved relatively popular, though buyers would tire of "bathtubs" by the early Fifties.

As it had with the Airflow, Chrysler Corporation went its own way for '49, fielding a crop of cars that were efficiently packaged but deadly dull. This approach reflected the personal preferences of company chairman K.T. Keller, who insisted on chair-height seats and sufficient interior headroom to accommodate a man wearing a hat. He got what we wanted. Today it's referred to as "three-box design": a passenger compartment "box" with engine and trunk "boxes" tacked on. Body lines were predictably angular, and the shorter-wheelbase lines, namely Dodge and

Plymouth, ended up looking stubby and awkwardly foreshortened. Hoodlines were prominently higher than the front fenders on all models, though the fenders blended into the main structure per postwar fashion. Rear fenders were much narrower but still visually distinct forms. Though practical and comfortable, the '49 Chrysler products lacked the styling excitement buyers were looking for, and by 1952 the firm would surrender its place as the industry's number-two producer to a rapidly recovering Ford Motor Company.

Besides those already mentioned, the Forties witnessed several other developments that would influence the course of American car design. Advances in glass-making spurred adoption of curved rear windows and one-piece windshields on certain car lines. The decade also saw the decline of wood as a structural body material, though not before several limited-edition wood-body specials appeared to spruce up their makers' carryover 1946-48 lineups. They included the Ford and Mercury Sportsman convertibles, Nash's Ambassador Suburban fastback sedan, and Chrysler's Town & Country fleet. All-steel

wagons began arriving for 1949 to replace traditional woody models and their extra expense and maintenance problems. Chevy, Pontiac, Olds, and Plymouth's De-Luxe Suburban lead the way. Ford and Mercury were the last to abandon the woody, for 1952. The superior strength and lower cost of steel combined with a

Opposite page, top: Lincoln's 1949 Cosmopolitan convertible, another "bathtub." Bottom: Chrysler's 1946-48 Town & Country (convertible shown) was the most elegant of the early postwar non-wagon woodies. (Owner: Roy Bleeke). This page: 1949 Buick Roadmaster Riviera (top) and Olds 98 Holiday (Owner: Woody Hyde) pioneered the pillarless hardtop.

steady middle-class migration to the suburbs to raise the station wagon to new heights of popularity in the Fifties.

But it was the pillarless "hardtop convertible" that was destined to be the single most popular postwar body style. It arrived for 1949 with a trio of GM offerings: the Buick Roadmaster Riviera, Cadillac's Series 62 Coupe deVille, and Oldsmobile's 98 Holiday. Interestingly, Chrysler had considered a hardtop for its 1946-48 Town & Country series, then decided against it after building seven prototypes, leaving GM to claim another styling first. The idea was hardly new. Sedans with removable center or "B" pillars had been seen way back in the late Teens, and the removeable "carson top," a popular accessory for

Twenties roadsters, prompted thoughts of capturing a convertible's top-up look with a fixed, metal superstructure. Buyers loved the hardtop's combination of open-car airiness and closed-car practicality, and it wasn't long before designers began snipping the center roof posts from four-door sedans and even wagons.

With rapidly rising production in the boom economy of the early postwar years, the auto industry had pretty much disposed of the wild and woolly seller's market by 1949. But the general economic expansion continued into the Fifties, and Americans remained in an expansive mood despite trouble on the international scene. The Depression was now a distant memory, and more people than ever could

afford to indulge themselves in very visible ways. As one of the most conspicuous of consumer goods, the automobile naturally reflected this mood, which explains why car design in this decade was increasingly dominated by a kind of cosmetic trendiness, almost the exact opposite of "form follows function." The result was a profusion of styling gimmicks that served no real purpose other than to make each year's model look as different as possible from the previous year's—and, of course, the competition. Among the decade's more dubious design developments were wraparound windshields with knee-banging "dogleg" A-posts, proliferation of more garish colors in two- and even three-tone combinations, constantly swelling fins, a

panoply of scoops and scallops, and tasteless slabs of chrome "put on with a trowel," as Bill Mitchell later recalled.

It was also a time of dramatic annual change, a big reason so many collectors are attracted to these cars today. As an example, consider Chevrolet's swift and striking styling switch from the sober conservatism of 1954 to the cartoonish effrontery of its 1959 "bat-wing" model. Even now, it's hard to believe a mere five years could separate two designs of such vastly different character.

With the end of the seller's market, the industry's few remaining independent producers found themselves increasingly hard pressed by the Big Three, particularly after 1949, and fighting harder than ever to survive. Though they ultimately lost the sales war, some managed to score a few styling triumphs. One of the most memorable was the second-generation Kaiser, introduced for 1951. Shaped by Dutch Darrin with an assist from Duncan McRae, it was sensationally low and curvy—rakish, clean, beautifully balanced. Boasting a relatively large greenhouse on a compact lower body, it claimed the greatest glass area in the industry prior to Chrysler Corporation's 1957 cars, and the lowest beltline, too. The windshield and rear window were curved, and provided instant identification via an unusual "sweetheart" dip in their upper edges. Ornamentation was restrained, with a crisp horizontal-bar grille and, on costlier versions, a simple, wide rub molding along the lower bodysides. Inside were ample room for six, a stylishly swept-away dash, and the broad palette of colors and trims associated with K-F's imaginative interior designer, Carleton Spencer.

In all, the "Anatomic Design" Kaiser was a knockout. And that, ironically, con-

tributed to K-F's ultimate demise. At a time when chrome-laden barges were all the rage, the clean and curvaceous Kaiser somehow wasn't "hot" enough. Neither was the performance of its aging L-head six in a market gone crazy for high-power V-8s. A couple of major management miscues only accelerated the company's decline, and the Kaiser marque disappeared from the U.S. scene after 1955. But the car itself lived on—in Argentina no less—all the way through 1962, a tribute to the inherent "rightness" of its design.

Nash scored a styling coup of a different sort with an all-new 1952 senior line bearing the signature of famed Italian designer Battista "Pinin" Farina. A vast improvement over the dumpy Airflyte, the new design employed a "three-box" format with artfully smoothed edges and corners. Retained were the unusual skirted front and rear wheel openings, which tended to

make the cars appear they were floating on air. A full-length sheetmetal crease just above these helped break up the plain sides, while a one-piece windshield, wraparound rear window, and thin aluminum window frames helped lighten upper body appearance. Farina would apply these same touches to the 1953 edition of Nash's pioneering compact Rambler to similarly good effect. Though the firm would never get around to convertibles and station wagons in its senior line, it did field a hardtop coupe. Alas, this generation would prove to be Nash's last stand. After merging with Hudson in 1954 to

Opposite page: 1951 Kaiser (Deluxe shown) was low and lithe. (Owner: Arthur Sabin) Above: Nash's '52 Ambassador Super by Pinin Farina.

form American Motors Corporation, Nash garishly facelifted the Farina platform through 1957, after which the make disappeared for good.

If Nash had merely used a famous name to evoke European elegance, Studebaker actually achieved it with one of the single most acclaimed designs in U.S. automotive history. It bowed for 1953 as the Starlight pillared coupe and Starliner pillarless hardtop, offered in both six-cylinder Champion and V-8 Commander guise. Again, the artistic hand of Raymond

Loewy was evident, though team member Bob Bourke contributed mightily to making this whole greater than the sum of its parts.

Sensationally low and riding an unusually long 120-inch wheelbase, the "Loewy coupe" was a model of tasteful restraint. Its shapely nose was flanked by two simple horizontal slots bisected by single thin bars, and Bourke gave the ensemble a lighter look by moving the bumper up slightly and adding a contoured valence or "modesty" panel below.

Compared to others cars' massive chrome "smiles," this Studebaker front seemed positively delicate. Bodysides were mercifully free of doodads, but visual interest was provided by a sculptured character line that mimicked the shape of the side window area and was faintly reminiscent of the Classic era's "LeBaron sweep." The greenhouse itself was light and airy, with a sharply raked one-piece windshield, fairly slim pillars, and a wraparound rear window. Completing the package was a clean tail with modest vertical taillamps.

Ford Motor Company instituted another corporate-wide overhaul for 1952, producing a group of lower and wider cars that nevertheless managed to look stubbier than their 1949-51 predecessors. One-piece curved windshields and wrapped backlights appeared across the board. Bodies were now fully slab-sided except for a raised, rear fender sub-form that was angled foward at its leading edge and capped with vertical chrome moldings that suggested air scoops. Grille design reflected the price and prestige pecking order, with Ford having the simplest treatments and Lincoln the most elaborate.

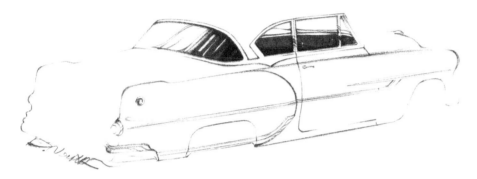

Gimmicky roof treatments fascinated Dearborn designers in these years. The first in production appeared for 1954 on the Ford Crestline Skyliner and Mercury Monterey Sun Valley. Both were two-door hardtops with a green-tinted Plexiglas panel instead of steel for the forward half of the roof. This novelty was intended to give front seat passengers the feeling of being "comfortably out of doors," but excessive interior heat buildup made the cars anything but comfortable on sunny days, and they sold poorly. The feature returned for 1955, when a jazzy facelift brought wrapped windshields and bulkier, reshaped sheetmetal for both makes. The Skyliner gave way to the new Fairlane Crown Victoria, also offered with a full steel roof. This was not a hardtop but a club sedan cleverly disguised with a brushed-metal wrapover roof band that hid the B-pillars. Mercury dropped its Sun Valley for '56, but the Crown Victoria continued for one more year, with the plexi-top model still finding very few takers.

GM's primary styling innovation in this period was the wraparound—or what it called "Panoramic"—windshield. While

Opposite page, top: 1952 Lincoln Capri hardtop coupe. Note raised rear fender form. Bottom: "Smiley" front, beltline dip marked Buick's 1953 Skylark. (Owner: Joseph E. Bortz) This page, top: 1953 Studebaker Starliner hardtop (Commander shown) and pillared Starlight coupe were among the decade's best designs. Raymond Loewy was responsible. Above left: 1954 Pontiac Star Chief Catalina. Above right: 1952 Mercury Monterey.

Some of Detroit's best styling in the Fifties appeared for 1955, that banner year when most every make broke all previous sales records. Perhaps the best of all was a totally new Chevrolet—clean and classic.

severely curved rear windows had been in use for some time, achieving optical clarity of sufficient quality for a windshield at acceptable cost required a tremendous investment in new production technology. As the nation's largest automaker, GM was best able to afford it.

The wrapped windshield was part of the "aircraft" style so beloved by Harley Earl. The feature had appeared on several show cars before the firm decided to offer it on a limited-production basis for 1953. The first to get it were Chevrolet's new fiberglass-bodied two-seat roadster, the Corvette, and a pair of convertibles based on standard volume bodyshells, the Oldsmobile 98 Fiesta and the Cadillac Series 62 Eldorado. For 1954, the firm's senior B- and C-body lines—Buick, Cadillac, and Oldsmobile—were completely restyled to incorporate the wrapped windshield. At the same time, they picked up blockier, slab-sided contours, with the hood and front fenders almost even in height. The new look proved quite popular. Buick was rewarded for its efforts by ousting a still-staid Plymouth from third place in industry sales.

Some of Detroit's best styling in this decade appeared for 1955, that banner year when most every make shattered all its previous sales records. Perhaps the best of all was a totally new Chevrolet, which also boasted a milestone new V-8 engine that forever banished the make's solid-but-stolid image. Along with division sibling Pontiac (which also got its first-ever V-8 this season), the '55 Chevy used GM's new A-body, with the expected wraparound

front glass and true "envelope" shaping. But while the Pontiac was simply busy, the Chevy was classically handsome. Its all-star design team comprised Clare Mac-Kichan, Chuck Stebbins, Bob Veryzer, and Carl Renner, who worked under Harley

GM's 1954 "Panoramic" wraparound windshield.

Earl's dictim of "go all the way, then back off." The result wasn't as radical as it might have been, but it wasn't far off. Better still, it bore no ties at all to the dull 1953-54 models despite using the same 115-inch wheelbase. Notable highlights were a rectangular Ferrari-like eggcrate grille, a fashionable show-car-inspired beltline dip, graceful rooflines, a tidy tail, and just enough ornamentation to attract the eye without offending it. A front fender sheetmetal crease extended back from the newly hooded headlamps into the door area, capped by a simple chrome molding on top-line Bel Air models. An angled vertical molding dropped from the beltline notch to a horizontal rear quarter "spear" molding to delineate the contrast-color area for two-toning, which also encompassed the rear deck. The combined tail and backup lamps rode high on the rear fenders and were visible from the sides. Overall, the '55 Chevy was attractively trendy, yet avoided the excesses that marred so many of its contemporaries.

A late arrival in the 1955 Chevy and Pontiac lines proved to be the year's most innovative new body style. Called Nomad at Chevy and Safari at Pontiac, it was a dashing two-door "hardtop" wagon, with a roofline borrowed from a 1954 Motorama show car derived from the production Corvette. Its main elements were wide B-pillars raked forward toward the top, plus side glass curved at the rear corners so that the usual D-pillar was effectively

combined with the liftgate frame. Rear-sliding windows were used immediately aft of the door glass in place of conventional wind-down panes, and the tailgate/liftgate was raked forward to carry the roofline smoothly down to the back bumper. Full-width groves were cut into the rear half of the top, the artifact of a planned tele-scoping section that was quickly axed by high production costs.

Beautiful and unusual though they were, the Nomad and Safari proved im-practical for wagons (water leaks around the sloped liftgate were a common prob-lem), and high prices put a further damper on sales. Both models were dropped after 1957, though their names continued for many years on more ordinary wagons.

Chrysler Corporation had been on a steady decline since 1949, and styling—or rather the lack of truly attractive styling—was clearly a big part of the problem. Not even the growing performance reputation of its high-efficiency hemispherical-head V-8, introduced for 1951, could turn things around. But help was on the way. K.T.

37

Keller became company chairman in 1950. Succeeding him as president was Lester Lum "Tex" Colbert, and one of his first moves was to schedule a corporate-wide redesign for 1955 at a projected cost of some $100 million.

Meanwhile, design director Virgil Exner was collaborating with Ghia in Italy on a series of interesting show cars that deftly blended some of the Classic-era touches he favored with the coachbuilder's mastery of European form. These exercises influenced the new '55 look a great deal. From the low-priced Plymouth to the now-separate Imperial marque, all Chrysler makes employed wrapped windshields, with the A-posts slanted forward to avoid the "doglegs" of Ford's vertical and GM's reverse-angle pillars. Exner personally supervised development of the senior lines—DeSoto, Chrysler, and the luxury Imperial—entrusting Plymouth and Dodge to colleague Maury Baldwin. Together they produced a contemporary and fresh-looking group of cars that stood in sharp contrast to Keller's "boxes." Naturally they were longer, lower, and wider, but they were also more colorful and had a much stronger sense of "direction." The last was emphasized the following year

with more prominent rear fenders, the finned "Forward Look" that soon had more buyers flocking to showrooms than dealers had seen in years. On the strength of its 1955-56 models, Chrysler made a dramatic sales recovery while strongly challenging GM as the industry's style leader.

But it was only a warmup. In an unprecedented break with Detroit's usual three-year design cycle, Chrysler spent $300 million on yet another top-to-bottom styling overhaul for 1957. This time, Exner and company really outdid themselves. The new models were lower than anything else on the road, with markedly wedge-shaped profiles taken in part by the aptly named Ghia-built Dart show car of 1956. All hood and front fender ensembles were now virtually flat. Beltlines plunged and glass areas grew accordingly. Rooflines were graceful, almost delicate on hardtop coupes. Though there was a strong family relationship among the five makes, each was individual and imaginative in execution, with Plymouth and Chrysler being arguably the cleanest and most arresting of the bunch. Plymouth's 1957 ad slogan accurately described the impact of the new styling by announcing, "Sud-

denly, It's 1960!" And with cars that made most everything else seem either garish or old-fashioned, it seemed Chrysler had indeed leap-frogged the competition. Unhappily, the stylists got carried away beginning with the 1959 models, and Chrysler was again plagued by unpopular styling in the early Sixties. This time, though, its cars weren't too conservative but too bizarre, and it nearly cost the company its shirt.

Apart from the last, Studebaker-based 1957-58 models, all Packards of the Fifties were built around designer John Reinhart's "high pockets" bodyshell, introduced for 1951. It was a big improvement on the old "pregnant elephant," but it wasn't exactly beautiful and it aged rapidly. After revitalizing Hotpoint appliances, hard-charging James J. Nance took over from Hugh Ferry as Packard president in early 1952. Nance knew something had to be done, and he ordered chief stylist Richard A. Teague to do it.

He did a masterful job. Working around the shallow "high pockets" greenhouse, Teague managed a fashionably wrapped windshield by cutting doglegs into the doors. Then he added a mammoth grille, hooded the headlamps, dressed up the flat bodysides with jazzy chrome trim, and capped it all off with distinctive "cathedral" taillamps above rear bumper exhaust outlets. The result was contemporary and looked all-new, even though it wasn't. But it arrived too late to do much for Packard's rapid downhill slide. Production tie-ups and mechanical bothers did the rest. Still, the '55s and the little-changed '56s are memorable as the last "real" Packards and the first with V-8 power.

Ford Motor Company borrowed many of its late-Fifties styling themes from recent show cars. The first to arrive was an all-new 1956 Lincoln with a front end lifted largely from the wild Futura, which then lent its huge canted tailfins to the facelifted '57 Lincolns. Likewise, the '57 Ford owed its rakish vee'd side trim to the experimental Mystere of 1955, while its fully flat hoodline, fall-away grille, and prominent headlamp housings had been previewed by the Lincoln X800 showmobile. With lower, sleeker, and jazzier looks, plus a wide model lineup spanning two different wheelbases, Ford nipped Chevrolet in

model year production for the first time since 1935.

The most blatant example of "dream car design" was actually advertised as such: the 1957 Mercury. Inspired by the XM Turnpike Cruiser, it was gimmicky, glittery, and gadgety, with very angular lines that made it more distinct from Ford than any Mercury in years. At the top of the line was the new Turnpike Cruiser series, which had just about everything: "sky-light dual curve windshield," dummy air intakes over the windshield corners for housing radio antennae on two- and four-door hardtops (a convertible was the only other offering), and a retractable, reverse-slanted rear window. Despite all the Tomorrowland stuff, the Cruiser failed miserably, as did the rest of the Mercury line. While it could be said that today's kitsch was high style in the Fifties, cars like this were too far out even for that gilded age.

Opposite page: 1955 Plymouth Belvedere hardtop coupe, styled by Maury Baldwin. Above: Virgil Exner's 1955 Chrysler C300. (Owner: Richard Carpenter) Below: 1957 Chrysler 300C convertible.

While the last "real" Packards were being built, Ford's fascination with unusual roof designs led to development of a convertible with an electric retractable hardtop. It appeared for 1957 along with the "latest expression of 'dream car' design."

A far more enduring and tasteful design appeared for 1956 with the Continental Mark II. In fact, it was one of the decade's best. John Reinhart, recently arrived from Packard, and Gordon Buehrig of Auburn-Cord-Duesenberg fame were primarily responsible for this latter-day classic, with elegant long-hood/short-deck proportions thoroughly evocative of Edsel Ford's timeless 1940-41 "Mark I." Like the hallowed original, the Mark II still looks good today—exceptionally clean and dignified without being stuffy. Only the mildly wrapped windshield dates it. The Mark II also introduced a distinctive identification point that would be passed down through successor models and is still with us today: the humped trunklid, recalling the first Continental's exterior-mount spare tire.

Ford's fascination with unusual roof designs led to development of a convertible with an electrically retractable hardtop as part of the Mark II program. For cost and time reasons, the idea ended up in the '57 Ford line as the Fairlane 500 Skyliner. This model seemed to offer the best of both worlds: the top-down good looks and driving fun of a fully open convertible and the superior weather and crash protection of a sedan. But though the Skyliner wowed crowds with its fancy "disappearing act," the retracting mechanism was complicated and usually unpredictable in operation, and this plus nearly nonexistent luggage space led most buyers to conclude that the car really wasn't worth its considerable price. Company president Robert S. McNamara wasn't fond of such tricks anyway, and he personally decreed the end of this slow-selling model after 1959.

The '57 Ford and Mercury platforms became the basis for a much-ballyhooed new medium-price make launched for 1958: Edsel. The product of exhaustive market

This page, top: 1955 Packard Four Hundred. (Owner: Harold Gibson) Above: Mercury's gimmick-ridden '57 Turnpike Cruiser hardtop sedan. Opposite page, top: 1956-57 Continental Mark II. Bottom: Ford's '57 Skyliner retractable in action.

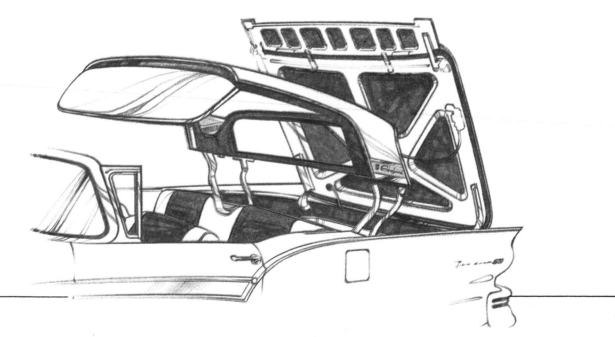

The new '57 Ford and Mercury formed the basis for the much-ballyhooed but ill-fated new medium-priced Edsel, still remembered mainly for its "horse-collar" grille and as a spectacular flop.

research begun back in 1954, it arrived with the start of a deep economic recession that caused the total market to contract, with the biggest losses occurring in the medium-price field. Had it actually been the radical new car some had predicted, Edsel might have made it. But it was just another middle-class model: no worse, but certainly no better, than its rivals—and not all that different from the Ford and Mercury that sired it. Worse, Edsel was handicapped by uninspired styling supposedly aimed at the "young executive on the way

up." A vertical grille theme was chosen to help establish the new make's identity, which it did in an unintended manner. Easily the most controversial aspect of the entire design, it drew damning descriptions like "horse collar," "toilet seat," and "an Oldsmobile sucking a lemon." With all this, Edsel was doomed from the start. After grimly hanging on for two more model years as little more than a Ford variation, it was consigned to history for lack of interest.

General Motors gradually resumed its

role as industry styling leader, but not before it had inflicted a garish group of 1958 models on a public fast tiring of planned obsolescence and wretched design excess. Harley Earl seldom misjudged buyer tastes, but he did this year, when GM's often heavy use of chrome reached a new high. Buick and Oldsmobile were the biggest dazzlers.

For 1959, something else reached a new high at GM: fins. Management's decision to institute closer divisional body sharing brought a completely restyled corporate fleet that replied directly to Chrysler Corporation's 1957 initiative—and rendered the all-new 1958 Chevrolet and Pontiac platforms instantly obsolete. The emphasis shifted from chrome to contouring as all GM makes became noticeably lower and considerably wider. Designers saved their wildest ideas for the top and bottom of the line. Cadillac took on towering tailfins made all the more outlandish by projectile-like taillamps. The '59 Buick was almost as contrived, sprouting a large, canted blade either side of a sloped rear deck. Oddest of all was Chevy, with a flat rear deck "large enough to land a Piper Cub," as veteran road tester Tom McCahill put it. At the trailing edges were "horizontal fins" turned down toward the center in a French curve and surmounting huge "cat's eye" taillamps. Oldsmobile adopted "The Linear Look," with a visually expansive full-width grille and concave back panel. "Rocket" ornaments atop each front fender were continued as chrome moldings to the rear fenders, which were scalloped just below to create a "jet-trail" effect at the fender ends. This left a new "wide-track" Pontiac with the company's most tasteful looks. Up front was a new divisional trademark, a split grille formed

by two wide ovals laid on their sides. A longitudinal vee'd groove in the center of the hood was repeated on the rear fenders as small twin fins canted opposite each other.

Giant windshields and novel rooflines were featured throughout the '59 GM lineup. Front glass was compound-curved, wrapping up the top as well as the sides. (This feature marked the '59 Mercury and Chrysler Corporation's 1957-58 convertibles.) Two-door hardtops wore slim-pillar superstructures, with roof area greatly reduced by much taller backlights and the upward-arcing windshields.

Opposite page, top: Ford's '57 Fairlane 500 hardtop sedan. Bottom: 1958 Edsel Pacer hardtop sedan. (Owner: Edsel Ford) This page, top: The '59 Cadillac 62 displays its outlandish fins. (Owner: Joseph Linhart) Center: 1957-58 Cadillac Eldorado Brougham nose and tail. Above left: 1957 Plymouth Fury's "shark" fins. Above: 1957-58 Imperial, with "gunsight" taillamps and dummy rear deck "tire."

GM's 1959 compound-curve windshield

A surprise development was two different hardtop sedan styles: a "flat-top" version with a radical wraparound rear window and a slight bit of overhang at the roof's trailing edge, and a six-window type with a more conventional curved roofline and small triangular panes just aft of the doors.

Before leaving the Fifties, we must note the growing influence of European sports cars on the American public and, inevitably, American car designers, for this trend would blossom in the Sixties. Its seeds had been planted right after World War II, when low-slung two-seat roadsters like the Morgan, MG TC, and Jaguar SS100 were brought home by GIs returning from England. Fun to drive, lithe and raffish in character, and full of "exotic" features like bucket seats, floor-mount gearshifts, and arcane "erector-set" folding tops, they generated a lot of interest while attracting a small but vocal group of enthusiast owners. The arrival of more modern designs like the Triumph TR2 and Jaguar's speedy, sexy XK120 only increased the public's sports car fascination.

At first, sports cars were only a minuscule presence in the U.S. market, but demand became consistent enough by the early Fifties to encourage two major producers to issue one of their own. Chevrolet was first with the Corvette, which went into limited production in late 1953 after causing quite a stir earlier that year as a Motorama experimental. Its body was

made of the new fiberglass material, but the chunky, high-waisted lines quickly earned the nickname "plastic bathtub." The Corvette also drew barbs for its curious combination of the futuristic and the traditional. Sports car purists were put off by the jazzy styling (especially the rocket-motif taillamps) and lack of a manual gearbox (two-speed Powerglide automatic was the only transmission offered), while more comfort-conscious, boulevard cruiser types didn't like the clumsy snap-in side curtains or the performance of Chevy's old "Stovebolt six." High price and a confused marketing plan made buyers wonder whether Chevy was really serious about the Corvette, and only 4629 were called for through model year 1955.

Ford handily avoided these problems with its two-seat Thunderbird, announced for 1955. Styled by Frank Hershey and Bill Boyer, it was intended to be a "personal" car rather than a *pur sang* sports machine, arriving with proper roll-up windows, a conventional steel body, and a potent 292-cid V-8 available with either stickshift

or automatic transmission. Like Corvette, it sported a wrapped windshield, long-hood/short-deck proportions, and a definite American design flavor, yet it was arguably more graceful and fleet-looking. Today it's considered a modern classic. The Thunderbird easily outsold its Chevy rival right from the first (16,155 versus 674 for model year '55).

Even before the first two-seater had been built, Ford had already decided to turn the Thunderbird into a larger, plusher package that division chief Robert S. McNamara thought would be far more saleable. He was right. Arriving for 1958 was a four-seat model with closely-coupled square-cut body lines and an innovative interior with a control console running down the center, dictated by the high driveline tunnel that resulted from its step-down, unit-construction design. Instead of a convertible with an optional lift-off hardtop, the "Squarebird" offered two body types: a hardtop coupe with an angular, wide-quarter roofline that proved immensely popular, and a convertible with

Opposite page, top: First seen as a Motorama dream car, Chevrolet's new fiberglass-bodied two-seat Corvette went into production on June 30, 1953. Bottom: GM's "flat-top" 1959 hardtop sedan roofline. Above: 1955 Ford Thunderbird replied to Corvette with steel body, more amenities, and arguably nicer lines. It's a bona fide "classic."

1958 Ford Thunderbird hardtop roof

After a decade of fins, flash, and fripperies, Detroit returned to a more tasteful, enduring design aesthetic in the Sixties while responding to buyer demands with a variety of new sizes, models, and concepts.

a rear-hinged decklid that completely hid the top when stowed, an idea inspired by the Skyliner "retractable." Today, the first-generation four-seat Thunderbird is generally regarded as the first of the "personal-luxury" breed that would proliferate in the Sixties. Continued through 1960, the "Squarebird" easily outsold the two-seat 1955-57 models. The margin was nearly 2 to 1 in its first year alone.

Chevrolet responded to the Thunderbird by reworking Corvette into a genuine "race-and-ride" sports car. The transformation began with 1955 availability of a three-speed manual gearbox and the division's sensational 265-cid V-8. Then came a beautiful, brand-new body for '56. Still artfully rounded, it was better detailed and had a more ground-hugging appearance. Elliptical bodyside indentations, often called "coves," added visual interest in profile while strengthening the car's identity, and weather protection improved with the addition of standard roll-up windows and an optional lift-off hardtop. Together with markedly improved handling

and the potent V-8, this styling boosted Corvette model year production nearly fivefold. That volume then nearly doubled for the stylistically unchanged '57, where optional fuel injection and considerably more horsepower were the main attractions. Lasting just two years, the second generation would prove to be the shortest-lived Corvette of all, yet it assured the future of "America's Only True Sports Car." By 1960, its brighter, bulkier third-generation derivative had turned the profit corner, thus winning Corvette a permanent place in the Chevy lineup.

After a decade of fins, flash, and fripperies, the industry returned to a more tasteful, enduring aesthetic in the Sixties. At the same time, it responded to increasingly specialized buyer demands with a variety of new sizes and concepts.

Heralding these trends were the Big Three's first-ever compacts, introduced for 1960. A response to the growing popularity of the Rambler American and Studebaker Lark in the wake of the '58 recession, they were quite different from those

Below: Chevrolet's Corvette became a prettier and more serious sports car with Harley Earl's brilliant new 1956 design. Opposite page: 1958 Ford Thunderbird pioneered bucket-seat "personal luxury." Above: The pert 1960 Studebaker Lark convertible.

Left: Ford Falcon was the most orthodox of the Big Three's new 1960 compacts. Below: Chrysler's Valiant looked the most European. Opposite page: Chevy's trend-setting 1960 Corvair Monza coupe.

cars and each other. Ford's Falcon was the most conservative of the new trio, with a conventional six-cylinder drivetrain and simple body lines bereft of superfluous trim or creases. From its plain, concave grille to Ford's trademark circular tail-lamps, the Falcon looked to be exactly what it was: no-frills economy transportation. Chrysler Corporation's rival Valiant, on the other hand, was far sportier if almost as mechanically mundane. Virgil Exner endowed it with a longish hood and some of the "Euro-classic" touches he favored: large rectangular grille, blade-like fenderlines, fully open rear wheel cutouts, and a sloped tail with a dummy spare tire embossed in the trunklid.

Exner went on to apply the Valiant's basic look to a fleet of slightly smaller Chrysler Corporation products scheduled for 1962, but only the Dodge and Plymouth versions materialized. A management scandal in late 1960 ultimately precluded the proposed senior models (and also brought the end of DeSoto). It was probably just as well, for the "downsized" '62 Dodge and Plymouth sold poorly in a market not yet ready to embrace more rationally sized big cars. The upshot of the debacle was that Exner was forced to resign in 1962.

Chevrolet's Corvair was the most radical of the Big Three compacts because it was closest in concept to the increasingly popular air-cooled, rear-engine Volkswagen Beetle. Nevertheless, it was pert and practical, with a somewhat stubby,

grille-less nose, a simple perimeter character line on the upper bodysides, and a rounded rump. Initially, only a four-door sedan was offered, with greenhouse styling much like that of GM's big flat-roof hardtop sedans. Introduced at mid-model year was a two-door pillared sport coupe, with a shorter greenhouse and a correspondingly longer rear deck.

Though Corvair was not very successful as an economy car, it uncovered an entirely new market with the Monza, which also

bowed for mid-1960. This was essentially a jazzy version of the new coupe, adorned with a floor-mounted gearshift and vinyl-covered bucket seats that could have come from a European sports car. It proved an instant hit, bringing in the flood of orders that Corvair had so far failed to generate against the cheaper Falcon. With additional body choices for 1961 (including a new wagon), the Monza soon accounted for the bulk of Corvair sales, and would continue to do so through 1969.

Rival makes were quick to take note of the Monza, and buckets-and-console interiors soon began appearing in all sorts of cars, often teamed with more muscular drivetrains. Chevrolet set the pace for 1961 with the Super Sport performance and appearance package for its full-size Impala convertible and hardtop coupe; and Oldsmobile issued a glamorous bucket-seat droptop called Starfire that same season. Ford dolled up the frumpy Falcon with a Thunderbird-like interior to create the Futura, then embellished the package with a squared-up roof for "1962½." That was also the year that brought the first of Detroit's "intermediates," the Ford Fairlane and Mercury Meteor, and Chevy's belated conventional compact, the Chevy II. Naturally, there were sporty variants in all these lines from the start. None were exceptionally stylish, though, being mostly flat planes and sharp angles.

After nearly expiring in 1957-58, Stu-debaker had made a spectacular comeback with the compact Lark, a cleverly conceived update of its old 1953 sedan/wagon platform. But sales quickly tapered off once Big Three competition appeared, so newly named company president Sherwood Egbert called in Milwaukee designer Brooks Stevens to rework both the Lark and the aging Hawk coupe of 1956-61 on a crash basis for 1962. Though not a design triumph, the new Lark was certainly more attractive, and a bucket-seat Daytona hardtop and convertible arrived just to keep things interesting. The Hawk was something else. Stevens reskinned the old Loewy-styled hardtop, shaving off the now-dated fins and grafting on T-Bird-style square rear roof quarters. Renamed Gran Turismo Hawk, it was a remarkably tasteful and expeditious job accomplished for amazingly little money, and sales temporarily perked up.

The compact ranks swelled to 10 for 1961

with introduction of the Falcon-based Mercury Comet (actually a mid-1960 arrival); Dodge's duplicate of the Valiant, called Lancer; and a trio of front-engine GM models, the Buick Special, Oldsmobile F-85, and Pontiac Tempest. The last were arguably the best-looking small Detroiters yet, all six-window four-door sedans with prominent lower body sculpturing, neat hood/rear deck balance, and front-end themes obviously borrowed from each division's full-size models. Pillared and pillarless sport coupe derivatives soon followed, similar in general outline to the Corvair coupe, with the sportiest versions tagged Skylark, Cutlass, and LeMans, respectively.

For 1964 these cars were completely revised, with less adventuresome drivetrains and considerably larger dimensions that lifted them into the mid-size field. At the same time, Chevy added another nameplate to its growing roster with the

William L. Mitchell and his General Motors cohorts came up with two of the Sixties' most memorable design achievements. Both appeared for 1963: the elegant, broad-shouldered Buick Riviera and the sizzling Chevrolet Corvette Sting Ray.

Chevelle, a fourth version of this new A-body platform. The basic form on all was still essentially square, but bodysides were now gently rounded, wheel cutouts took on a more elliptical shape, and soft curves appeared in fenders and roof pillars.

The car that previewed this broad-shouldered look was one of the Sixties' stellar styling achievements: the 1963 Buick Riviera. A Ned Nickles concept executed under Bill Mitchell's guidance, this classy two-door hardtop was an inspired blend of Rolls-Royce and Ferrari themes. The former was evident in the elegant razor-edge roofline and smaller "formal" rear window. The latter was seen in a massive eggcrate grille set between ribbed vertical parking lamp housings originally intended to hide the headlamps, a change belatedly adopted for 1965. Lower body contouring was smooth yet crisp. A predictive feature was a marked sheetmetal bulge in the rear fender area just behind the doors, an early example of the "Coke bottle" look that would be one of the decade's biggest styling fads. The Riviera was GM's direct reply to the Ford Thunderbird in the burgeoning personal-luxury field. Originally developed as a possible LaSalle revival at Cadillac, it was turned over to Buick to bolster that division's sagging image, which it did superbly.

Mitchell and company came up with another *tour de force* for 1963: the equally timeless Corvette Sting Ray. Apart from sensational new styling lifted directly from Mitchell's Stingray sports racer of 1959-60, the big news was availability of the first closed Corvette, which ushered in another Sixties craze by reviving the fastback coupe body style last seen in the early Fifties. Common to both coupe and roadster was a lower body shaped like an in-

verted airfoil, with strongly peaked front and rear fenderlines, a pointed nose and tail adorned with blade-type split bumpers, and hidden headlamps. The last, incidentally, was another revival, the first time this feature had appeared in volume production since the '42 DeSoto. Bodysides were markedly tucked under below a peaked longitudinal character line running just above the wheel openings, and the old "cove" indentations gave way to simulated exhaust vents just aft of the front wheels. Another pair of dummy vents appeared on the hood, flanking a longitudinal bulge that was picked up on the coupe's roof as a dorsal "spine." This, in

turn, divided a large compound-curve backlight, producing what quickly became known as the "split-window" coupe. It was Mitchell's idea, but Corvette chief engineer Zora Arkus-Duntov thought the divider interfered with rearward vision. So did many buyers, and Mitchell reluctantly agreed to its removal on the 1964 and later models. In the overhead view, the coupe roof tapered toward the rear into a boattail, recalling the Auburn Speedsters of the Classic era.

Though the Sting Ray design lasted only five years, through 1967, it became progressively cleaner and meaner. By the end of the classic fourth generation, Mitchell's

Opposite page, top: Ford's blocky 1962 Fairlane, first of the intermediates. Bottom: Chevy's conventional Chevy II compact ('64 shown) was equally square-rigged. Above: 1963 Buick Riviera was a Ned Nickles concept originally slated to revive the LaSalle nameplate.

Above: Stunning '63 Corvette Sting Ray coupe boasted split rear window, peaked fenders, and evocative "boattail" roof taper. Doors cut into roof á la 1948 Tucker. Below: Elwood Engel's clean-limbed 1961 Lincoln Continental revived the production convertible sedan for the first time since 1951.

crew had removed all the non-functional doodads, while Duntov added such high-performance desirables as standard four-wheel disc brakes and optional 427-cid big-block V-8s offering up to 435 horsepower. Needless to say, these are now among the most prized Corvettes of all, the one-year-only split-window coupe in particular.

While GM cars became increasingly curvy and sensual, Ford Motor Company concentrated on a boxier look, with prominent fronts and square-edged lines that were gradually softened to achieve a kind of "important" bulkiness. The firm's best single design in the early Sixties was unquestionably the 1961 Lincoln Continental. A vast departure from the overblown and overdecorated 1958-60 models, this smaller luxury car was uncommonly clean and well detailed. Designer Elwood Engel specified a closely coupled passenger compartment and sporty long-hood/short-deck proportions, which he then adroitly balanced with the more formal air of rectilinear fenderlines discretely decorated with slim chrome moldings. Two novel throwbacks appeared here: a four-door convertible sedan, the first since Frazer's 1951 model, and rear-hinged "suicide doors," used here and on a hardtop-styled pillared four-door sedan, the only other body type initially offered. Up front was an unusual, finely checked convex grille, with a horizontal divider bar holding sunken-in dual headlamps at its ends. (The recessed lights also appeared on this year's all-new third-generation Thunderbird, which actually shared the Continental's cowl structure.) To its credit, Ford resisted the temptation to monkey

with this Continental's enduring simplicity, and it preserved this basic format as the make's design trademark until the mid-Seventies without cluttering it up. Once Engel moved over to Chrysler Corporation as Virgil Exner's successor, he applied bright-edged fenderlines and more upright architecture to a far more handsome Imperial for 1964, then to Chrysler and the full-size Dodge and Plymouth lines for 1965 and beyond. It was welcome relief after too many years of oddball styling from Highland Park.

Studebaker was losing the sales war badly in the early Sixties, but president Sherwood Egbert wasn't going to go down without a fight. He decided that Studebaker needed a daringly different car that would bring people flocking back to his mostly empty showrooms while bolstering the firm's image as a "going" concern. Trouble was, the new model was needed yesterday. Egbert put in a call to long-time company styling consultant Raymond Loewy, who moved fast, sequestering associates Robert F. Andrews, John Ebstein, Tom Kellogg, and Frank Spring at his Palm Springs home where they could work undisturbed. The team produced a finished ⅛-scale clay model (based on previous Loewy concepts) in less than a week. By April 1961, barely five weeks after the project had been initiated, a full-size clay had been completed and tooling orders were being placed.

The result was spectacular. Aptly named Avanti, which means "forward" in Italian, it was marked by a long nose, pinched-waist "Coke bottle" mid-section, wraparound rear window, and a bobbed rear deck. Some analysts decided there

wasn't a straight line anywhere on it, but they might have missed the raised "gunsight" panel placed asymmetrically on the left of the hood. There was no conventional grille; a simple open under-bumper slot was used instead. The smooth shape yielded superior aerodynamics decades before designers routinely thought about such things. Loewy had just guessed, but it showed how "right" the design was.

Unhappily for Studebaker, the Avanti launch was anything but right. Egbert's production hurry-up dictated a fiberglass body, but supplier problems produced poorly fabricated panels that delayed customer deliveries, thus blunting the public's high initial interest and reinforcing Studebaker's reputation as a "loser." A high price and competition from the stunning Sting Ray didn't help. By the time things got sorted out, buyers had mostly gone elsewhere. After building fewer than 4200 Avantis for 1963-64, Studebaker beat a hasty retreat to Canada and eventual extinction as an automaker. The Avanti would survive, however, thanks to South Bend dealers Leo Newman and Nate Altman. With Corvette power and a few other modifications, it continued as the largely custom-built Avanti II through the early Eighties. It's still with us (minus the Roman numeral) under the stewardship of Steven Blake.

Detroit's increasing emphasis on personal sportiness reflected the growing influence of the "youth market," the vast postwar "baby boom" generation that reached car-buying age in this decade. Winning the loyalty—and dollars—of this important new customer group was the main motivation behind two concepts that

appeared for 1964: the "muscle car" and the "ponycar."

The "muscle car" was more a marketing ploy than a new design direction, essentially the Sixties equivalent of the "horsepower race" in the Fifties. Nevertheless, the "performance look" proved extremely popular, and buyers began demanding the same air of aggressive power in cars with little, if any, "hot rod" pretensions.

Pontiac's GTO established the formula: a powerful, big-inch big-car V-8 stuffed into a smaller, lighter mid-size platform, with suspension, steering, and brakes suitably beefed up to handle the extra brawn. Conceived by Pontiac advertising executive Jim Wangers and division general manager John Z. DeLorean, the GTO was introduced as an option package for the bucket-seat Tempest LeMans coupe, convertible, and hardtop to get around a GM edict that precluded engines larger than 330 cid in anything but full-size models. It was a clever gambit and a super bargain. With a base price of between $3200 and $3500 and scorching performance from 389 V-8s offering 325 or 348 bhp, the GTO was a huge hit with would-be street racers, and Pontiac sold more than 30,000 of the '64s. Ironically, the division had expected to move only about 5000, and insiders say the actual total would have been much higher had more cars been available.

Despite its extrovert character, the first GTO was quite subdued. Visual distinction from run-fo-the-mill Tempests was limited to different nameplates, black-finish grille inserts, and two fake hood scoops. But the crouching stance and jumbo tires were dead giveaways, and they promptly became *de rigueur* for a slew of imitators that inevitably followed. Naturally, the GTO's styling followed Pontiac's now well-established "Wide Track"

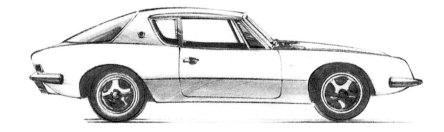

themes, which had helped boost the division to a solid third in industry sales by the mid-Sixties. Hallmarks included clean bodysides, near-full-width taillamps, semi-concealed via thin horizontal bars, and the distinctive split grille that had been around in various forms since 1959.

Ford's Mustang also inspired a herd of imitators, which the press soon referred to as "ponycars" in its honor. There was justice in that. As the first car designed specifically for the burgeoning youth market, it quickly became the sales phenomenon of the decade. Partly because its debut season was longer than the industry norm, Mustang shattered the previous record for first-year new-model sales at nearly 681,000 units to become the third most popular car line in the land.

Generally credited to Ford Division general manager Lee Iacocca, the Mustang was disarmingly simple in concept. Essentially it was a rebodied Falcon, sharing drivetrains, major chassis components, dashboard, and other hardware, clothed in sportier garb. The long-hood/short-deck styling was evocative of the two-seat Thunderbird, a revival of which had been briefly considered. Its most notable features were a high-set "mouth" grille, a slim blade front bumper ahead of a deep

"modesty" panel, a bodyside character line ending in a dummy air scoop just ahead of the rear wheels, and a simply cropped tail with prominent central fuel filler and neat outboard taillamp clusters. This design, the winner in an intramural competition involving several staff proposals, was principally the work of a Ford Division studio team comprising Joe Oros, L. David Ash, and Gayle L. Halderman. A 1.5-inch-shorter (108-inch) wheelbase left Mustang with less cabin and cargo space than Falcon, but most buyers didn't seem to mind. And Iacocca's insistence on a back seat, however cramped, proved a definite

sales plus. So did a vast array of individual accessories and option packages that allowed the basic Mustang to be highly personalized. A low starting price of just $2368 only encouraged buyers to pile on the goodies.

Mustang bowed publicly at the New York World's Fair in April 1964. Body styles were initially limited to the ex-

Opposite page: Raymond Loewy's dynamic 1963 Studebaker Avanti. Above: 1965 Ford Mustang, the first "ponycar." Top and left: Pontiac's '64 GTO "muscle car."

pected convertible and notchback two-door hardtop. A fastback coupe bearing the "2+2" designation arrived for the formal 1965 model year, identified by functional air extractor vents in place of rear quarter windows. Plymouth provided some immediate competition with a fastback of its own, the Barracuda. Appearing at about the same time as Mustang, it was not a direct rival, but it was close enough. Basically, it was Elwood Engel's "breadloaf" second-generation Valiant with a

sloped superstructure incorporating a huge, wrapover rear window. A proportionally stubbier front made Barracuda less graceful than Mustang, but it was just as practical and a little more versatile, and it sold well. By 1965, it was the single most popular model in the Plymouth line.

The styling highlight of 1966 was unquestionably the Oldsmobile Toronado. A personal-luxury coupe built on a big-car 119-inch wheelbase, it marked the return of front-wheel drive to American produc-

tion for the first time since the Cord 810/812 of the late Thirties. Body design, created by Olds studio stylist Dave North, was fully in keeping with the innovative mechanicals. A full fastback, it had an abbreviated "Kamm-type" tail and C-pillars melded in smoothly with the lower body. Uncommonly long front overhang served to emphasize the driven front wheels, and the whole thing was set off by aggressive full wheel openings with prominent "lips" or "brows." This new E-body

by a curious backlight curved in a reverse "S" configuration.

Detroit designers worked overtime for 1968. Normally cautious Chrysler Corporation completely revised its Dodge Charger to produce one of the year's most striking cars. The blocky 1966-67 fastback body gave way to a sleek notchback style, with a separate rear deck and a smooth "flying buttress" roofline, the latter so-called because of the sloped side or "sail" panels flanking an upright rear window. Though this and the humped fender contours were obviously borrowed from GM, Highland Park achieved an even slicker look by radically curving the bodysides and narrowing the fenders toward the front and rear in plan (overhead) view. It was the first expression of the new "fuse-lage" style that would prevail at Chrysler for the next several years. The firm's other intermediates also took on smoother lines. Among them was Plymouth's new Road Runner, which found a ready and willing market as the first "budget" muscle car.

Ford Motor Company also stressed intermediates for '68 with a stylish new

platform was also used for a completely restyled second-generation Buick Riviera, which retained rear drive and wore its own sleek outer skin. Cadillac then adopted the entire Toronado package for a brand-new interpretation of its high-line Eldorado. Introduced for '67, it had more formal lines, with Cadillac's typical broad eggcrate grille, crisper roof and fender contours, and a novel rear window vee'd in the center. The last idea would be applied to a whole raft of lower-priced GM coupes in the Seventies.

Model year 1967 also saw a major restyle for the original ponycar, and its first overt rivals. GM fielded a pair of divisional twins, the Chevrolet Camaro and Pontiac Firebird, with the same rakish proportions as Mustang but smoother "Coke bottle" body and fender contours. From rival Lincoln-Mercury Division came a plusher pony called Cougar. Riding a three-inch-longer (111-inch) wheelbase, it looked somewhat more elegant and expensive than Mustang. Notable was a distinctive dual-element grille with fine vertical bars

and hidden headlamps. This motif was repeated at the rear as chrome trim for the wide taillamps. Plymouth responded more directly to Mustang with a brand-new Barracuda bearing handsome Italianate lines that fully divorced it from the workaday Valiant. "Hippy" rear fenderlines were again in evidence. The fastback lost its wrapped rear window but gained convertible and hardtop coupe companions. The latter was distinguished

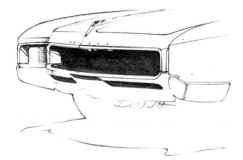

1966 Buick Riviera had hidden headlamps

Opposite page, top: Dodge's Charger fastback became this slick notchback for '68. Bottom: Oldsmobile's front-drive '66 Toronado had abbreviated beltline and long snout. This page, top: Chevy's curvy 1967 Camaro. Above left: Full-fastback '67 Mustang 2+2.

The Seventies saw the end of the muscle market and growing buyer preference for certain "neoclassic" styling features that came to connote status, elegance, and luxury.

Ford Fairlane/Torino and Mercury Montego/Cyclone. The highlight of these lines was a rakish fastback hardtop coupe inspired by the 1967-68 Mustang 2+2. Noses were rounded, wheel arches prominent, and back panels abruptly cut off in the now-familiar performance idiom, and an upswept rear side window line was employed to avoid rear-quarter heaviness. Some of these touches were dictated by aerodynamic considerations in long-distance stock-car racing, where the Big Three had been fighting fiercely since the early Sixties for victories that often made a big difference in showroom sales.

Mid-size models also stole the '68 spotlight at GM. In an unusual move, two-door models were given their own 112-inch wheelbase to give them a tighter, sportier

1970 Plymouth Road Runner Superbird

look compared with the 116-inch-wheelbase four-door sedans and wagons. Hardtop rooflines were slightly concave, and C-pillars dropped unbroken into the lower body, reflecting Toronado influence. External sheetmetal panels were unique to each member of this corporate quartet.

Pontiac's Tempest/LeMans was arguably the best of the bunch, particularly the sharp new GTO with a pointy body-color bumper/grille made of deformable Endura plastic.

AMC's belated entry in the ponycar field arrived for '68 as the Javelin, and Dick Teague pulled out all the stops to create a good-looking fastback hardtop that owed nothing to its rivals. Especially pleasing were the chunky, high-set tail, a slightly concave backlight (pioneered by Pontiac's personal-luxury Grand Prix of 1963), strong wheel arch forms, and a shapely nose announced by a bold "twin-venturi" split grille. As if this weren't enough, Teague cleverly sectioned the Javelin's central body a full 12 inches to create a nifty two-seater, the AMX, which bowed at mid-season. Though it never sold in high numbers and only lasted through 1970, this car showed just how resourceful the industry's smallest producer could be.

What would prove to be the longest-lived Corvette design also arrived for 1968 in the form of a rebodied Sting Ray. Previewed by the Mako Shark show car of 1965, this new fifth generation was marked by a pinched midsection, a closely cropped "Kamm" tail with a modest trailing-edge "spoiler" to smooth air flow, and a low nose jutting out between severely humped front fenders. Hidden headlamps were now joined by hidden windshield wipers (they came out from under a vacuum-operated panel in the cowl top when switched on). This feature also showed up on some of GM's 1968 full-size products. Alas, the boattail Corvette coupe was gone, but its replacement was an innovative notchback style with twin lift-off panels above the cockpit and a longitudinal divider bar between windshield header and a rear roof "hoop." It was the first T-bar roof, an idea that would find wide acceptance in the Seventies. It also likely hastened the demise of the fully open convertible.

The Seventies saw a growing public preference for certain styling features that came to connote status, elegance, and luxury. Together they defined a "neoclassic" or "neoformal" look inspired partly by the great Classics and partly by the trademark style points of several prestigious European makes, particularly Mercedes-Benz and Rolls-Royce. As a result, American car design in the Seventies was characterized by a broad return to much boxier body forms and widespread use of square, upright, Mercedes-style grilles, typically capped by "standup" mascots (hood ornaments) of the sort Detroit had mostly

abandoned in the Fifties. Wide-quarter rooflines with small back windows had gained favor in the Sixties for the air of moneyed privacy they conveyed, accompanied by the rise of vinyl coverings, a throwback to the leather-back styles of the coachbuilt era. The Seventies brought two futher roof embellishments, both dubious. One was "coach lamps," small running lights that glowed when the headlights were switched on, usually mounted on the B- or C-pillars. The other was a shrinking of rear side windows on some coupes and even some sedans, leaving slim, generally vertical panes popularly known as "opera windows." Fortunately, the public would begin tiring of such faddish fripperies by the end of the decade.

Decidedly unfortunate was the profusion of "battering ram" bumpers that appeared at mid-decade, the industry's clumsy first efforts at meeting the government's five-mph impact-protection standards that took effect for 1973 (front)

and '74 (rear). At about the same time, Congress appeared ready to pass a law governing occupant protection in a rollover situation. The threat turned out to be only that, but it gave automakers the excuse they'd been waiting for to drop their slow-selling convertibles, only to revive the body style a decade later. It also spelled the end of hardtop coupes and sedans, which were gradually replaced by fixed-pillar styles beginning with GM's "Colonnade" intermediates of 1973.

If the Seventies quickly degenerated

Opposite page: GM's 1968 mid-size two-doors rode a shorter wheelbase than four-door models. That year's slick Pontiac GTO (shown) wore a body-color plastic bumper/grille. This page, top: Designer Richard Teague sectioned AMC's '68 Javelin ponycar to create the two-seat AMX. Left: Chevy's smooth 1970 Camaro.

into the most boring decade ever for U.S. car design, they began with some of the most exciting machines in Detroit history. Heading the list was a peerless pair of ponycars with a basic shape so good that it would survive into the Eighties: the second-generation Chevrolet Camaro and Pontiac Firebird.

GM's 1967-69 ponycars had been compromised, according to Bill Mitchell, by sharing a higher-than-desirable cowl and shorter-than-desirable dash/front axle span with the '68 Chevy Nova compact. But there was no compromise here, and the result was nearly flawless: smooth, taut, and uncluttered, with excellent surface development that elegantly expressed GM's then-current styling philosophy of "stretching fabric over a wire skeleton and blowing air into it from the bottom."

Though both models shared the same F-body "anatomy," Chevy designer Henry Haga and Pontiac colleague Bill Porter conspired to give each its own distinct personality, mostly via carefully conceived front and rear sheetmetal. The basic platform was a smooth fastback coupe shell (low sales precluded a convertible this time), with an abbreviated tail, very long doors, and no rear quarter windows. Viewed from ahead or behind, the body sloped down and outward from the roof to a longitudinal mid-height character line, then tucked in sharply. Once again, there was no beltline break at the C-pillars, though careful sheetmetal shaping gave each car the appearance of having definite

"shoulders." Announcing Camaro was a simple rectangular grille flanked by single headlamps. The grille shell flowed back into a modest hood bulge, and combined with sculptured inboard front fenders to define small "catwalk" areas. Out back was a simple concave panel below the trunklid, with a central license plate mount and four circular taillamps arranged in pairs, Corvette-style. Firebird wore Pontiac's usual split grille with a prominent vertical "beak." The grille sections were deeply set into the grille frame, which was covered in body-color Endura plastic and doubled as the bumper, as on recent GTOs. Again, front fenders were formed at their forward ends to house the headlamps. Bringing up the rear was an angled panel with broad trapezoidal taillamps above the bumper.

The literal beauty of this design was that it proved to be easily adaptable to sub-

sequent styling changes dictated by federal requirements. It's one reason GM held onto its ponycars after rival companies had abandoned theirs. However, give full credit to the firm's skillful stylists for their deft interim facelifts, and to persuasive Camaro/Firebird boosters within GM, who successfully lobbied against plans to drop these models after 1974.

At American Motors, Dick Teague penned a smooth new compact to replace the aging Rambler American. Reviving the Hornet handle from Hudson days, it arrived for 1970 with quasi-ponycar proportions, prominent lipped wheel arches, clean sides, and straightforward front- and rear-end styling. A minor innovation was the "Sportabout," a sloped-back wagon with a jaunty air and a one-piece lift-up rear "door" or hatch. Recalling his successful Javelin-to-AMX surgery, Teague created a subcompact at low cost by simply slicing off the Hornet's tail, installing a rear liftgate window, and sweeping the beltline

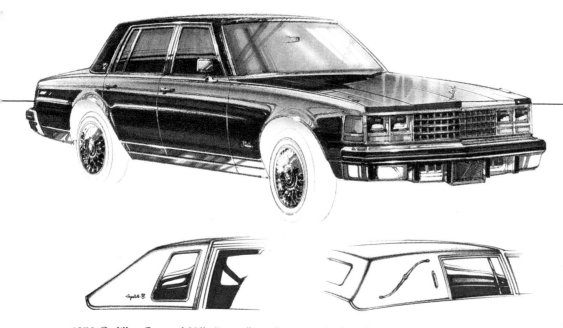

1978 Cadillac Coupe deVille "opera" window

Blind roof quarter with dummy landau bar

into the roof. Called Gremlin, it sold well through most of the decade (at least by AMC standards) despite the controversial styling. A variety of trendy trim packages aided its appeal with younger buyers. Teague also came up with attractive hatchback coupe styles in both lines.

The traditional full-size Detroit car had been rendered increasingly anachronistic by events of the early Seventies, and its days were clearly numbered by mid-decade. But though more buyers than ever were now willing to "think small"—or at least "smaller"—a great many did not want to give up big-car comfort and convenience just to get better fuel economy.

Thus was born the "luxury compact," which came to the fore in two new 1975 offerings. Serving the volume market was the Ford Granada/Mercury Monarch, a square-cut sedan and coupe originally developed to replace the 1970-vintage Ford Maverick/Mercury Comet. Upgraded at the last minute to fill the market gap Dearborn had detected, it was unabashedly

styled in the image of the junior "New Generation" Mercedes-Benz series, with a bit of extra "status" decoration ladled on. Advertising strived mightily to prove that these cars compared favorably with the vaunted German machines, which in some ways they did, yet sold for only a fraction of the price, which was definitely true A number of people literally bought this line, and the Granada/Monarch was one of Ford's more successful Seventies products.

Even more successful was the smallest Cadillac product since the last LaSalle. Reviving the Seville name from 1956-60, this heavily reengineered version of GM's corporate X-body compact bowed in the spring of 1975 as the most expensive offering in the Cadillac line, thus directly challenging the industry's time-honored notions about size and price. Styling was trim, tasteful, and conservative. More importantly, it effectively disguised the humble underpinnings. Notable were a right-angle rear roofline and a bolt-upright backlight (which would show up on a face-

lifted group of GM full-size cars for 1980), plus a scaled-down version of Cadillac's usual eggcrate grille and a dashing profile accented by full wheel openings. The Seville was effectively a trial balloon for GM's 1977 B- and C-body cars, the first phase of the revolutionary "downsizing" program the firm had been planning even before the oil embargo. Though it didn't oust the big Coupe de Ville as the most popular Caddy, it sold quite well—enough to prove that "snob appeal" wasn't necessarily a function of bulk and glitz, something foreign-car aficionados had known all along.

By the end of the Seventies, General Motors had shrunk its full-size, intermediate, and personal-luxury cars and had fielded a more competitive import-fighter in the Chevrolet Chevette. Chrysler Corporation continued to lose ground, though it did manage to come up with the industry's first small cars with front-wheel drive, the "two-box" Dodge Omni/Plymouth Horizon hatchback sedans of 1978. Copied almost line for line from Volkswagen's pace-setting Rabbit, they weren't *objets d'art*, but they were practical people-movers, and they literally kept Chrysler alive during the bleakest period

Opposite page, top: Lincoln's big and baroque Continental Mark IV was new for '72. Bottom: Third-generation Plymouth Barracuda for 1970 was smooth but meaty. This page, top: Cadillac's compact 1976 Seville, a downsizing trial balloon. Left: The clean, crisp 1979 Ford Mustang.

in its history. Obviously, smaller cars were the wave of the future, even if they inevitably cost more than the bigger models of old.

Ford Motor Company filled out the forecast with a brand-new Mustang for 1979. In some ways, it was the best car ever to wear the galloping pony emblem. In its surface execution, downswept nose, ample glass area, and minimal ornamentation, it combined the best of contemporary American and European design thinking. No wonder: it originated with a team headed by Jack Telnack, who had supervised creation of the perky little Fiesta minicar for Ford Europe. Moreover, it was genuinely exciting, a refreshing change from the pudgy 1974-78 Mustang II

and a far cry from the "fat" Mustangs of 1971-73. At long last, Ford had returned to the sort of restrained, efficient, and elegant ponycar it had built in the first place, yet the new model was roomier and weighed about the same. It also offered a more rational balance between performance and economy and better all-round roadability, reflecting the engineering progress of the intervening 15 years.

The '79 Mustang gave every sign of having been styled in the wind tunnel. And indeed, designers all over Detroit were rediscovering the science of aerodynamics in the quest for better fuel economy through reduced air drag. An optional turbocharged four-cylinder engine combined V-8 power with economy-car fru-

gality, thus underscoring the sort of advanced technology that would also be a part of our automotive future.

But most of all, this Mustang was a timely signal that Detroit had not forgotten about exciting cars—or what they looked like. The Eighties has so far witnessed a variety of interesting new models with the kind of style and substance that some people thought the industry had lost forever. We haven't seen the end of such cars, and there's a new generation of talented young designers already hard at work on even better ones for tomorrow.

So the design evolution of the American automobile continues, as vigorous and promising as ever. And from where we sit, it's only just begun.

Glossary of Styling Terminology

"A" PILLAR
The foremost pillar in the upper side structure of a vehicle. Successive pillars rearward are labeled "B", "C" and, on station wagons, "D".

ACCENT STRIPES
Fine, painted lines applied in contrasing colors to the finished body to accent certain lines and contours.

APPLIQUÉ
A decorative panel applied to a basic interior or exterior panel. May be metal, plastic, or a combination, with a bright, brushed, textured or painted finish.

ARGENT FINISH
A silvery, aluminum-pigmented paint with approximately the same color and luster as brushed or satin-finished chrome, aluminum or steel.

ARMATURE
Metal I-beam frame and wheels with a wood structure, and sometimes styrofoam, used as the base for a clay model and made approximately three inches under the size of the proposed finished clay shape. (Also called clay buck.)

"B" PILLAR
Second pillar in roof, counting rearward from the windshield.

BACKLIGHT
The window across the rear of any automobile regardless of body style. Also called back window and rear window.

BEAD MOLDING
A molding with a small cross-section and of any length.

BEAUTY BOLTS
Exposed, large, round, bright bolt heads on the surface of bumpers. Also used to identify similar parts of station wagon simulated-wood side treatment. The term "beauty" is used in this context with inverted humor.

BELTLINE
The line established by the upper edge of the car lower body at the glass openings, as seen from the side.

BEZEL
A frame, escutcheon, or rim, usually surrounding a lamp or opening. Either bright-finished or painted.

BISCUIT
Rectangular sewn area on a seat or door panel.

BLADE
A thin, shaply defined ridge in the body metal, or an appliqué of a similar nature.

BLIND QUARTER
An unusually wide "C" pillar or roof quarter tending to enclose rear seat area.

BLIPS
Small ornamentation in series; i.e., several identical ports, bars, windsplits, etc., aligned horizontally or vertically on the body.

BOLSTER
The portion of the seat that rolls over or forms the uppermost part of the seatback or the leading edge of the seat itself.

BRUSHED FINISH
Fine, directional disruption of a smooth surface. Usually done on aluminum, stainless steel, or chrome plate, but can be simulated in plastic.

BUCKET SEAT
Individual seat, often contoured so as to provide lateral support.

BUSTLEBACK
Conventional automobile configuration as differentiated from a fastback. Also termed notchback.

BUTTERFLY
Two pieces of wood joined together in the shape of a cross and used to carry clay.

"C" PILLAR
Third pillar in roof, counting rearward from the front.

CAMERA-CASE FINISH
A textured, leather-like finish used in car interiors, as on a glovebox door. The name is derived from the dark-grained leather used on expensive cameras.

CASTING
The shape formed by pouring or spraying a plastic or liquid substance into a mold and letting the material harden. Also used to describe the process itself.

CATWALK
A depressed surface, usually between a fender and a raised area of the hood or deck.

CENTER LINE
The plane passing through the center of a headlight, wheel or the vehicle itself.

CHAMFER
A flat surface beveled or angled off from an adjacent surface.

CHARACTER LINE
A line on the basic shape, resulting in an intersection of planes and sometimes ornamented.

COBBLED
Production car with experimental or design components added or substituted. Often used to describe a component or model put together quickly.

COKE BOTTLE
A double swell in the plan view contour. Looking directly down on a car, the body is narrower in the middle section than over the front and rear wheels.

CONVERTIBLE BOOT
A covering, usually held in place with snap fasteners, over the folded-down soft top.

CONVERTIBLE STACK
That part of a convertible top which projects above the beltline or deck when the top is folded down.

COWL
The portion of the body bounded by the front fenders, the base of the windshield, and the rear edge of the hood.

CUBE
Three-dimensional representation of the allowable dimensions for a vehicle under development. Also a grouping of exterior die models arranged in their proper position to check continuity of surfaces.

CURING
A stage required by some synthetic materials after forming and before further use.

CUTLINE
A groove etched in a clay model to represent a door, hood, or decklid opening.

CV WINDOW
Controlled Ventilation. A movable glass pane directly aft of the "A" pillar and separate from the side window.

"D" PILLAR
Vertical or diagonal structural pillar between roof and body at the rear corner of a station wagon.

DASHBOARD
A board on the fore part of a buggy or other vehicle to intercept water, mud or snow. Sometimes used as a synonym for instrument panel.

DECAL (DECALCOMANIA)
A decorative or informative transfer sheet used for wood graining, labeling, etc.

DECKLID
A hinged panel providing access to the luggage compartment.

DIE CASTING
Injection of molten metal under pressure into a fully finished mold. Also the product of such a process. Greater detail and more intricate shapes can be obtained with die castings than with stamped parts.

DIE MODEL
A three-dimensional representation made of hard wood from approved engineering drawings and aluminum templates.

D. L. O. (DAYLIGHT OPENING)
Line defining the areas through which light will pass in glazed areas.

DI-NOC
Trade name for a decal, material consisting of three layers, decal, glue and paper. The outer portion can be painted with a special elasticized paint. When applied to the surface of a model, the Di-Noc is first soaked in warm water. The wet paper backing is separated from the decal, which takes the form of the clay surface and gives the model the effect of a painted car.

DOGLEG
A right-angle bend, as in the angle made by the side and bottom of windshields of the mid-Fifties.

DRAG TEMPLATE
A pattern or guide of a particular of the body section (bumper, molding, etc.)

DRIP MOLDING (DRIPS)
An exposed channel applied to the roof over the side windows to direct water away from the windows and to cover structural welding. (See also gutter).

DRIVEABLE MODEL
A Fiberglas body mounted on a chassis and used to evaluate the model in motion.

EGGCRATE
A complex grillework made of intersecting planes, usually with more depth than can be obtained by stamping.

ELEVATION
Two-dimensional drawing of vehicle viewed from front, side, or rear.

ESCUTCHEON
An exposed panel or part used to retain, or to hide the retention of, another part; e.g., keyhole.

EXTRUSION
A part or component formed by pushing material (clay, plastic, metal) through a die by pressure, e.g., a molding.

EYEBROW
A cowl or visor above a headlamp, instrument panel or wheel opening.

FASTBACK
A roofline that slopes directly down toward or to the rear bumper of the vehicle.

FILLET
Curved surface used to blend two intersecting planes.

FISH HOOK
A spear- or arrowhead-shaped ending to a decorative molding or paint stripe.

FLANGE
A rib or rim that provides strength, guidance or a means of attachment to another object.

FOILED BRIGHT SURFACE
Bright aluminum foil applied over clay to simulate chrome-plated areas.

FWD
Front-wheel drive; engine and drive axle mounted at front end of chassis. (Not to be confused with four-wheel drive: 4wd).

GARNISH MOLDING
The upper molding on the door panel above the armrest, usually metal, used as a retainer for the door trim panel. Also found on "A" pillars, roof rails and backlight.

GRAN TURISMO
A closed two-seat coupe designed for rapid, comfortable touring with good performance and handling (in English, "Grand Touring").

GRAVEL DEFLECTOR
A metal plate fitted between the front or rear bumper and the body.

GREENHOUSE
The upper body of an automobile; the structure above the beltline—glass, roof, and supporting members.

GRILLE
An ornament designed to decorate an opening and to allow passage of air or sound.

GUTTER
A channel for water drainage. (See also drip molding).

HARD TRIM
The parts of the interior which are not soft trim; i.e., ornaments, garnish moldings, script, appliques, etc.

HARDTOP
A term applied to any fixed roof with retracting window glass and no exposed "B" or middle pillar.

HEADER
The structural member above the windshield at the juncture with the forward edge of the roof panel.

HEADLINING
The trim on the ceiling inside a car, usually vinyl but sometimes cloth.

HIGHLIGHT
Theoretically a path of light described by the intersection of a curved surface and a line or plane becoming tangent to that surface at a constant angle, usually 45 degrees.

HOOD
A hinged panel providing access to the engine compartment.

HOP-UP
An upward change of direction of a surface or line.

HUBCAP
A decorative disc covering the hub of the wheel, lug nuts, etc. (See disc & wheel cover).

IDIOT LIGHTS
Warning lights on an instrument panel which glow red when something in the engine goes wrong, e.g., low oil pressure.

INSTRUMENT PANEL
The portion of the interior extending from door to door directly in front of the driver and containing primary gauges and controls for operating the vehicle.

INTAKE
An opening in the surface to allow air to flow in, usually to cool brakes, engine, or occupants for passenger comfort.

JOUNCE CLEARANCE
Clearance between wheel and wheelhouse.

KICKPAD
The area along the bottom of a door interior, which is likely to be scuffed when getting in and out of a car.

KNOCKOFFS (OR KNOCKOFF HUBS)
Large wing-nut used to retain a wheel for rapid attachment or removal of racing wheels. Sometimes ornamental only.

LANDAU BAR
A decorative, S-shaped ornament located on the "C" pillar surface. Originally a functional S-curved hinge that allowed the rear part of the roof of a horse-drawn carriage to be folded down.

LAP JOINT
An overlapping joint, usually solder-filled unless covered by a molding.

LIP MOLDING
A bright molding applied to the sheetmetal around the edge of a wheel opening.

LOUVER
A fin that controls the flow of air through an opening. May also be non-functional in a simulated opening.

LOWER BACK PANEL
Portion of body sheetmetal below rear edge of decklid.

MAGS
A wheel cast in magnesium, then machined for attachment to hub, etc. Used primarily for racing because of extremely light weight, but sometimes used or simulated to add a racy appearance.

MODESTY PANEL
Sheetmetal below bumpers that conceals chassis members. Also called modesty skirt.

MOLDING
A strip of material either sunken or projected and usually decorative.

OGEE
A long, S-shaped curve.

OSCAR
The two-dimensional movable manikin used by designers and engineers to represent the size and shape of most drivers or passengers and the limitations of their movements.

OVERHANG
Distance from center line of wheels to rearmost (or foremost) projection of vehicle.

OVERLAY
A sheet of translucent paper laid over an original drawing to sketch an alternate version or design. Used for comparing two or more designs.

PACKAGE, PACKAGE DRAWING
—Package—concept or organization of vehicle including dimensions.
—Package Drawing—guide for use by engineering and design functions in completing design of total vehicle.

PACKAGE TRAY
The shelf-like portion of the interior between the top of the rear seat and the backlight.

PEAK LINE
An intersection of two planes, or a sharply defined ridge in a metal surface.

PILLAR
A vertical structural member connecting the upper roof with the lower body.

PLAN VIEW
A view looking down on the subject.

PLATEAU
A surface extending above the normal sheet metal.

POD
A streamlined compartment to house various mechanical implements; e.g., lights, dials, gauges, etc. It is usually round or elliptical.

POINTS
Exact locations on a model, usually derived from a blueprint or from the model itself to duplicate the opposite side of the model.

PORK CHOP
An extension of the instrument panel shape on the door, usually an integral part of the door garnish molding.

PROVEOUT MODEL
A clay model developed to verify surface drawing conformation with the appearance of the model originally approved by management. A record cast subsequently is made in Fiberglas. (See record model.)

QUARTER PANEL
1. A sheetmetal stamping; originally called a rear fender.
2. A sheetmetal panel encompassing the area from the rear door opening to taillight area, and from the rear wheel opening to base of roof and trunk opening.

RAMP ANGLE
Angle created by lines tangent to the static loaded radii of front and rear wheels, converging at the point of lowest ground interference of underside of car—angle of overhang at lower extremities.

RECORD MODEL
A Fiberglas or plaster reproduction of the original clay model as approved. (See proveout model.)

RENDERING
A detailed illustration.

RESIN
A plastic liquid chemical. The two most commonly used are epoxy and polyester.

REVEAL MOLDING
A metal frame or molding outlining an opening or depression.

ROCKER PANEL
The sheetmetal surface below the door opening, running between front and rear wheel openings.

SCOOP
A device to catch air; may be either functional or merely ornamental.

SCRAPER
A clay-modeling tool used to rough in the surface of a model and shaped like a short-handled rake with a straight or curved blade crosswise to the handle. The blade can vary from one to six inches wide. It has two sharpened sides, one of which has serrations or teeth and the other a smooth edge.

SCUFF PLATE
Cover over door sill, usually rubber or metal.

SEAT SIDE SHIELD
A metal or plastic molding or appliqué on the outer edge of the seat cushion and, in some cases, the seatback.

SEATING BUCK
A mock-up of a car's interior used to evaluate entrance and egress, seating room, comfort, instrument accessibility, etc. Dimensions are usually accurate to plus or minus .03 inch. (See trim buck.)

SECTION
View of any component at 90 degrees to a plane cut through the component.

SEDAN
Two-door or four-door car having stationary window frames in its doors.

SHEETMETAL
All areas of a car not glass, bumpers, grille, lights or trim that comprise the body; i.e., hood, fenders, quarter panels, instrument panel, decklid, etc.

SHIM STOCK
Extremely thin metal pieces used as dividers in the making of a mold.

SLICK
A thin piece of plastic with the edges ground free of all nicks and scratches. It is used to:
1. Smooth a clay surface.
2. Smooth aluminum foil onto clay or Fiberglas to simulate chrome trim on bumpers, moldings, etc., and to apply Di-Noc.

SOFT TRIM
The soft or yielding portions of an interior; i.e., seats, door panels, carpets, headlining, armrest, padding, etc.

SPLINE
A straight-edged stick or board of varying widths and thicknesses ranging from a foot to 12 feet in length; used to assist in finding low or high spots on the surface of a model.

SPOILER
An air deflector used on high-speed cars to control lift tendencies.

SPUD
A tool about 2 to 2½ feet long with a flat steel chisel edge, used for heavy digging or clay removal.

STUB PILLAR
Rear-door hinge pillar concealed behind and below beltline on four-door hardtops; a pillar that extends only from the rocker panel to the beltline.

SUGAR SCOOP
A depressed surface leading to an air scoop.

SURFACE PLATE
A flat cast-iron plate with five-inch grid lines inscribed; used as a base to take all dimensions.

SURPANEL
An extra panel adjoining a main panel, as in the sheetmetal under the grille and between the front fenders. (See modesty panel.)

SWEEP
A plastic, metal or wood guide used in drawing an irregular or flowing contour.

TAPE DRAWING
An outline of a car made with black, pressure-sensitive tape, which can be easily seen, removed, and changed. Most often depicts the side elevation.

TEMPLATE
An acurate surface profile taken from a blueprint or portion of a model to be duplicated. Can be made of cardboard, plastic, Masonite, plywood or metal, depending on proposed use.

THEME SKETCH
A quick sketch to get an idea on paper; precedes a rendering.

TREAD
Distance between the centerline of front or rear tires measured at the ground.

TRIM BUCK
A full-size model of an interior to show the design of a specific model. (See seating buck.)

TUMBLEHOME
Angle of the "B" pillar and side glasss from the perpendicular at the beltline, as seen from front or rear.

TUNNEL
The hump in the floorpan that provides clearance for the driveshaft.

TURNUNDER
Opposite of tumblehome. The inward and downward sweep of sheetmetal from the widest point on a car down to the rocker panel.

UPPER BACK PANEL
Portion of body sheetmetal between backlight and decklid.

VACUUM PLATING
The deposition of metal on basecoated objects by evaporation of a metal, usually aluminum, under high vacuum. Used to simulate chrome or other bright finishes in automotive design.

VALLEY
A surface between two higher surfaces.

WASTEGATE
Louvers or textured grille that permits the exhausting of air. Can be either functional or ornamental.

WASTE MOLD
A negative mold destroyed or wasted in freeing the positive cast.

WHEELBASE (WB)
The distance between the front and rear axles, usually expressed in inches.

WHEEL COVER
An ornamental disc that covers the wheel of a car, mounted on the rim. Sometimes called wheel disc. (See also hubcap.)

WHEELHOUSE
The encasement around the front and rear wheels.

WINDCORD
A narrow cord that frames a door opening and serves to finish the edge and close the gap.

WINDOW MOLDING
Any molding that frames the window of a vehicle; usually stainless steel or bright finished.

WIRES
Wire wheels or wheel covers that simulate wire wheels.

WRAPAROUND
Any surface that goes laterally across the car and around a corner, i.e., wraparound windshield, bumper or taillights.

ZERO LINE
Horizontal and vertical base lines from which all dimensions are taken.